Sign Language
CONVERSATIONS
for beginning signers

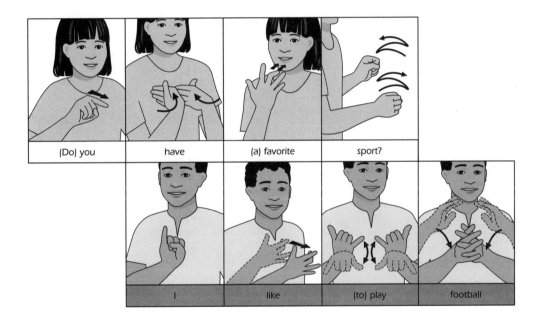

| (Do) you | have | (a) favorite | sport? |
| I | like | (to) play | football |

Illustration and design by
Jane Schneider and Kathy Kifer

A Breath of Fresh Air
GarlicPress

Dedicated to Emily, Elena & Jane.

Published by:
Garlic Press
605 Powers St.
Eugene, OR 97402

www.garlicpress.com

Table of Contents

Chapter 1

Introduction to Signing

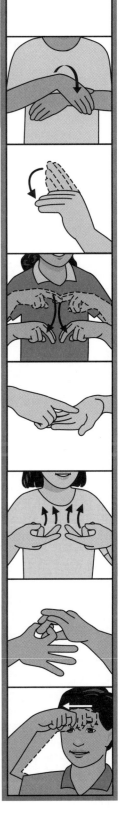

Sign Language Conversations has been written for beginning signers. It has a conversational style, introducing new vocabulary and accompanying activities. Each chapter introduces a topical subject and models a conversation. Following the conversation is an activity that is not only for enjoyment but also adds new vocabulary.

Conversations are patterned in Standard English with some simple variations. While the conversations and activities use English word order, the signs are largely from American Sign Language (ASL). This approach has been selected as the best bridge between deaf and hearing people.

When we say that Standard English word structure is presented with simple variations, let us explain.

If we were to hold to strict Signed English, conversations would sign each and every word as if in a speaking conversation. The conversation would use the inflections and verb tenses to match regular English speech.

For example:

Signed English

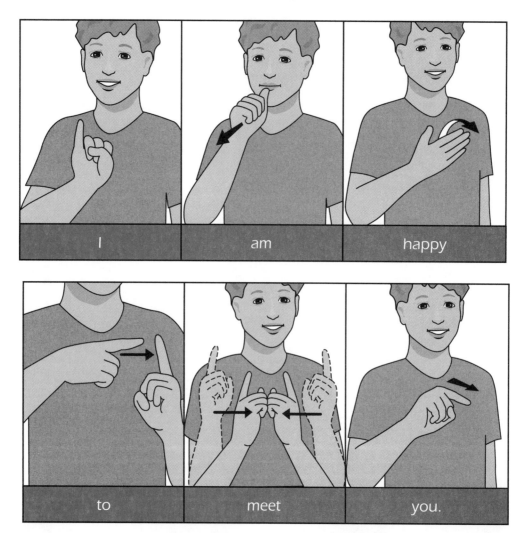

I	am	happy

to	meet	you.

Where	were	you	born?

If we were to hold to strict American Sign Language (ASL), our conversations would be much different. The order of words change and many words that would normally be spoken would be dropped. ASL uses the addition of facial expressions and body gestures to replace spoken words.

For example:

ASL

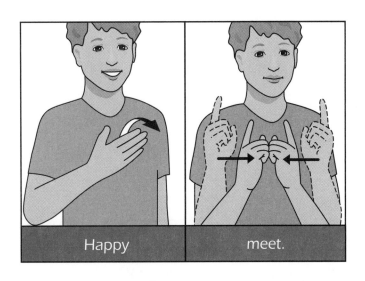

Happy   meet.

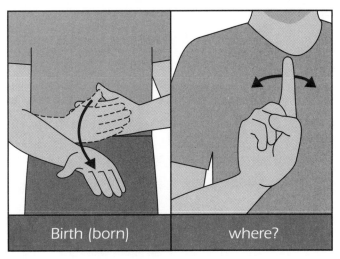

Birth (born)   where?

While this book does not model the word order of ASL, it does encourage facial expression, gestures, and the willingness to flatten tenses and drop small words. Our usage for this book is sometimes called Conceptually Accurate Signed English.

For example:

Our Usage

| I (am) | happy | (to) meet | you. |

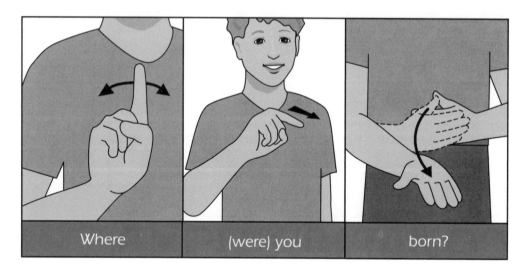

| Where | (were) you | born? |

Above all, this book encourages deaf and hearing to communicate. And in what better way than to foster the exchange between young signers?

Chapter 2

Fingerspelling

The Manual Alphabet is a standard for finger signs used to represent each letter of the alphabet. It is an important way to communicate, especially for new signers. The Manual Alphabet is most commonly used to fingerspell proper names and places, as well as words which simply do not have signs.

Fingerspelling helps new signers who may know only a few signs to keep a conversation going despite their limited knowledge of signs.

Let's introduce you to the Manual Alphabet in three stages and, at the same time, give you a chance to apply what you are learning.

As you learn and use the Manual Alphabet, try to move from letter to letter in a smooth, gliding manner. Avoid jerky motions. In the instance of words having double letters (like tree), move the second letter to one side in a slight bouncing motion:

t   r   e   e

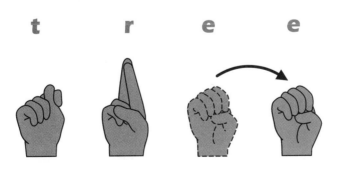

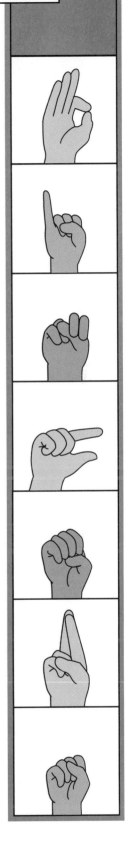

9

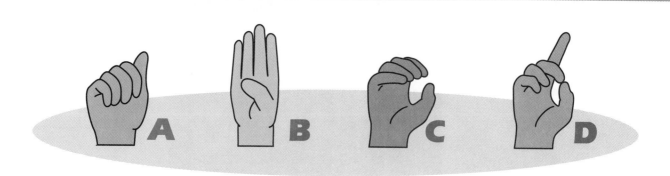

What signs are these?

Match the letter signs with their written alphabet letters.

D G E A F B H C

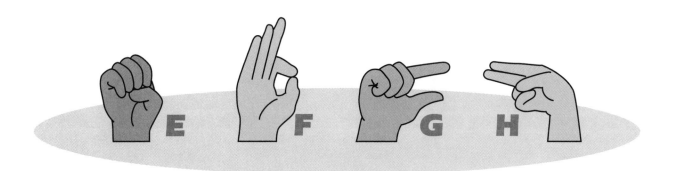

E   F   G   H

Can you identify these words?

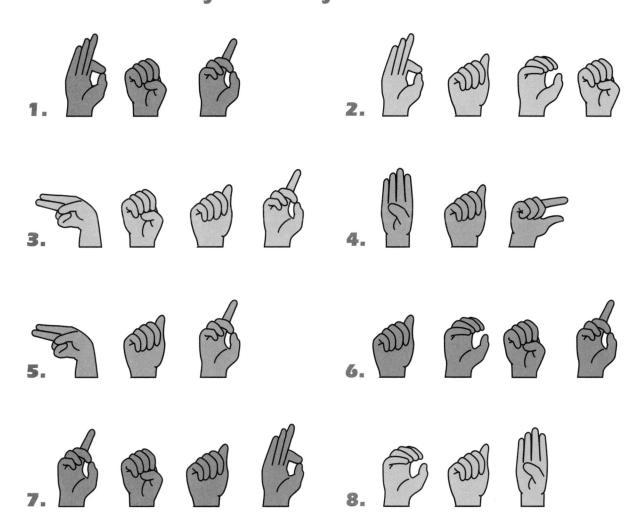

1.

2.

3.

4.

5.

6.

7.

8.

Activity: Practice A to H with a friend. Sign any two letters for a friend to interpret. Sign two consecutive letters. Your friend follows with the next two consecutive letters.

What signs are these?

Match the letter signs with their written alphabet letters.

N Q M P O K L J I

Can you identify these words? (no Q words)

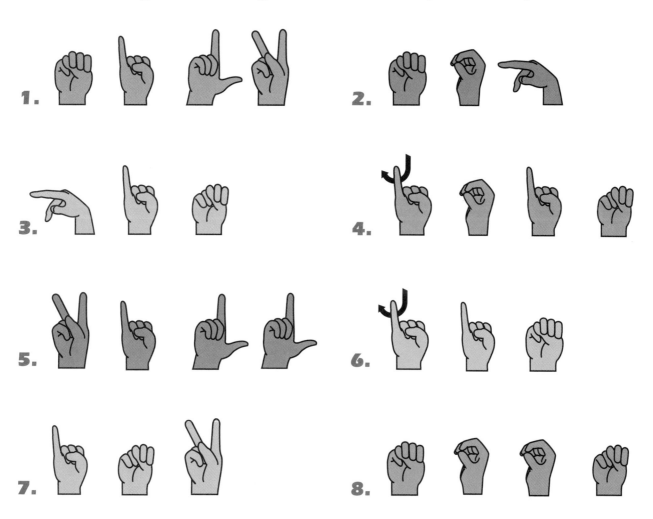

Activities: Use all the letters you have learned so far: Sign any 2 letters for a friend to interpret. Sign two consecutive letters. Your friend follows with the next two consecutive letters.

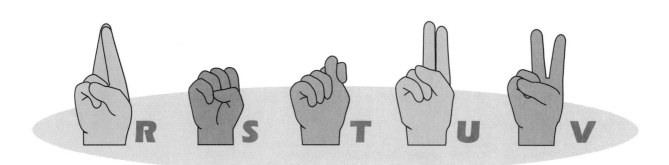

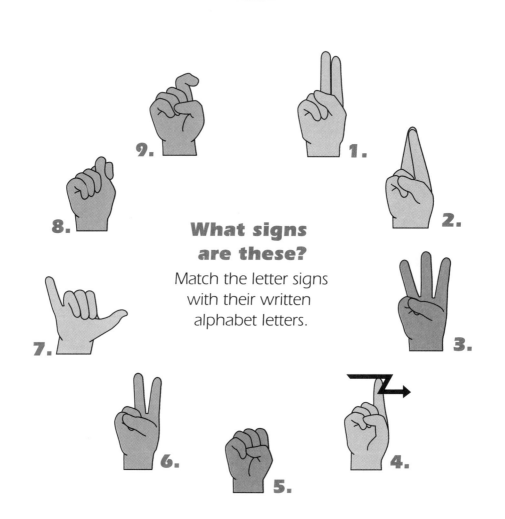

What signs are these?

Match the letter signs with their written alphabet letters.

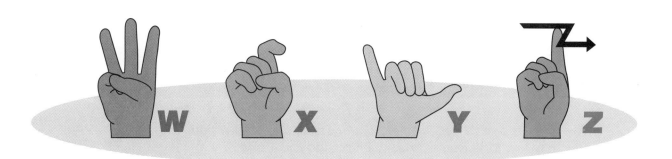

Can you identify these words?

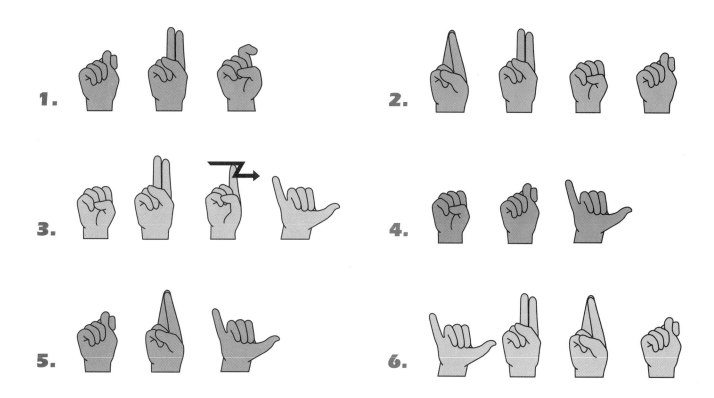

1.

2.

3.

4.

5.

6.

Activity: You now can finger spell anything that you can spell. Finger spell your name. Finger spell short words for your friend to interpret.

Fingerspelling Game

This game is best played with a group. Each player in turn signs the phrases to follow (one, some, or all), completing the answer by fingerspelling. The other members of the group translate the finger spelling.

Phrases:

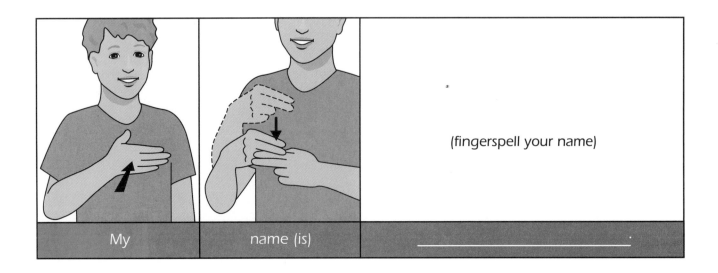

My	name (is)	(fingerspell your name)

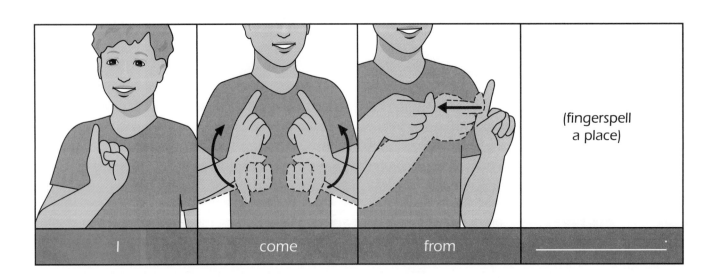

I	come	from	(fingerspell a place)

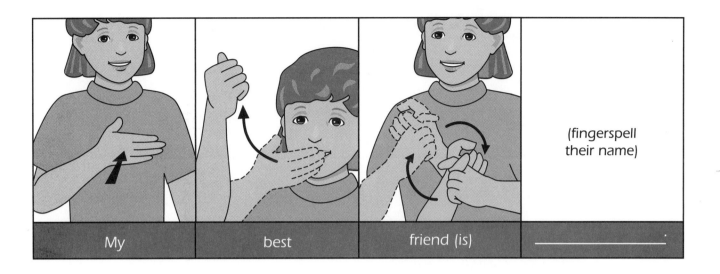

| My | best | friend (is) | (fingerspell their name) _____ . |

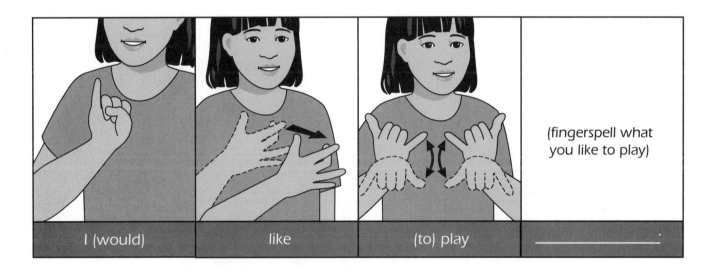

| I (would) | like | (to) play | (fingerspell what you like to play) _____ . |

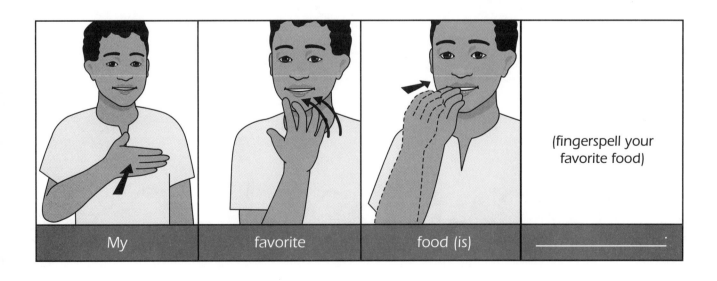

| My | favorite | food (is) | (fingerspell your favorite food) _____ . |

Change the answers to the phrases you have just learned, for example:

Fingerspell funny variations.

or

Fingerspell truthful answers.

or

Fingerspell creative answers.

or

Fingerspell through the alphabet:

For instance, My name is A-l-e-x. I come from A-l-a-s-k-a. My best friend is A-l-i-c-i-a. I like a-i-r-p-l-a-n-e-s. My favorite food is a-v-a-c-a-d-o. The next player would use B letters, the next C letters, and so on.

Or, making it more challenging: My name is A-l-f-r-e-d. I come from B-o-s-t-o-n. My best friend is C-a-l-v-i-n. I like to play d-o-m-i-n-o-e-s. My favorite food is e-g-g. The next player would begin with F letters, and so on.

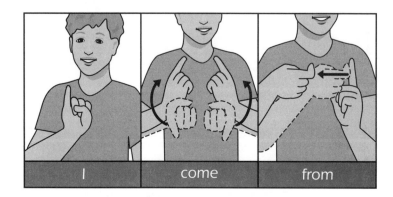

| I | come | from |

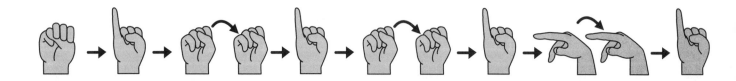

Chapter 3

Getting Acquainted

Hello.

My

name (is)

K - y- -l - e (finger spell the name)

What (is)

your

name?

My

name (is)

M - e - g (finger spell the name)

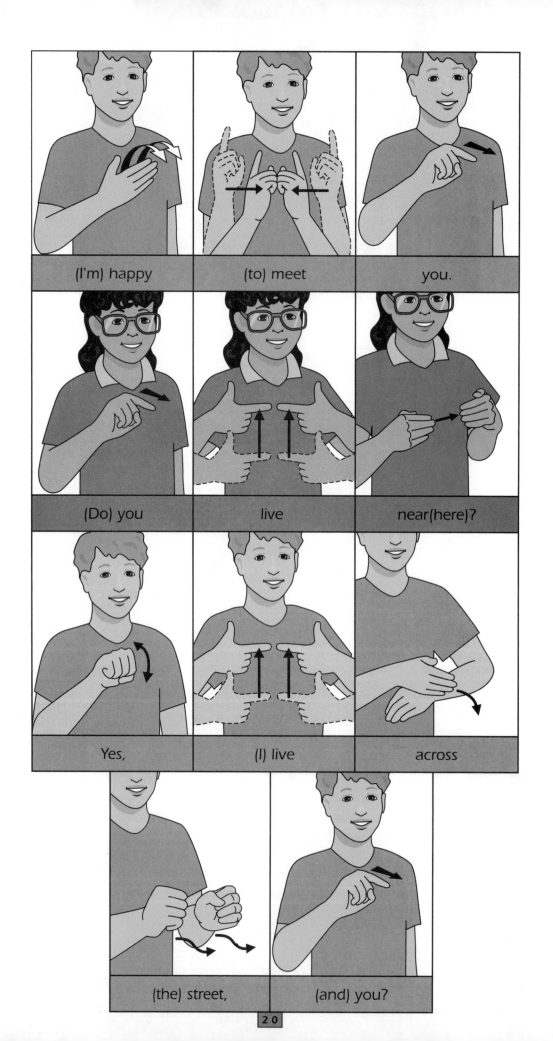

(I'm) happy	(to) meet	you.
(Do) you	live	near(here)?
Yes,	(I) live	across
(the) street,	(and) you?	

My   family   (and I) live

north   (of) town.

I   think   (I) know

your   brother.

No,   I   have   (a) sister.

How   old (are)   you?

I ('m)   almost   12 (years)   old.

Me   too!

| You | sign | well. |

| Thank | you, |

| I | practice | a lot. |

| Please | sign | more | slow(ly). |

All right. | Excuse | me,

(it's) time | (for) me | (to) go | home.

Nice | meet(ing) | you.

Good-bye. | See | You | later!

Here are various signs, letters, and symbols. When they are combined,
they present a word or phrase you should know. A hint is provided.

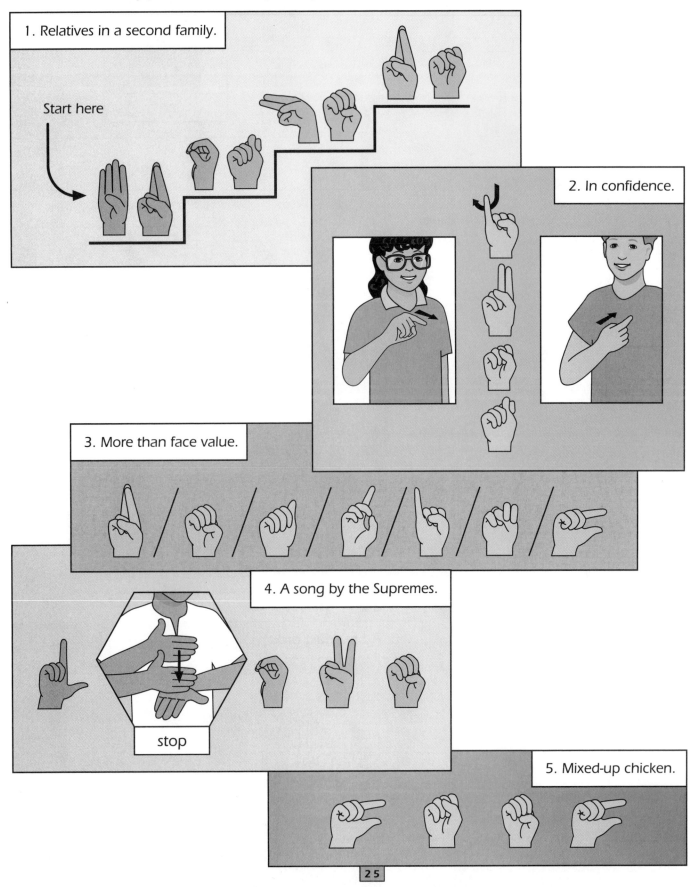

1. Relatives in a second family.

Start here

2. In confidence.

3. More than face value.

4. A song by the Supremes.

stop

5. Mixed-up chicken.

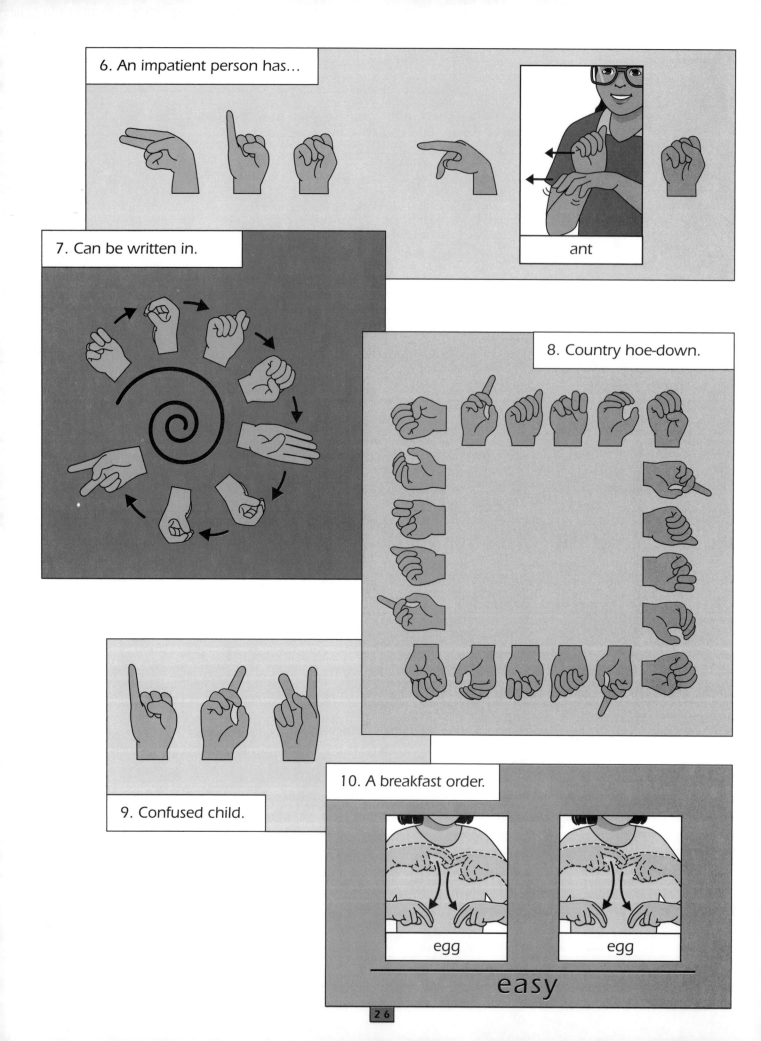

6. An impatient person has...

ant

7. Can be written in.

8. Country hoe-down.

9. Confused child.

10. A breakfast order.

egg

egg

easy

Chapter 4

Family and Friends

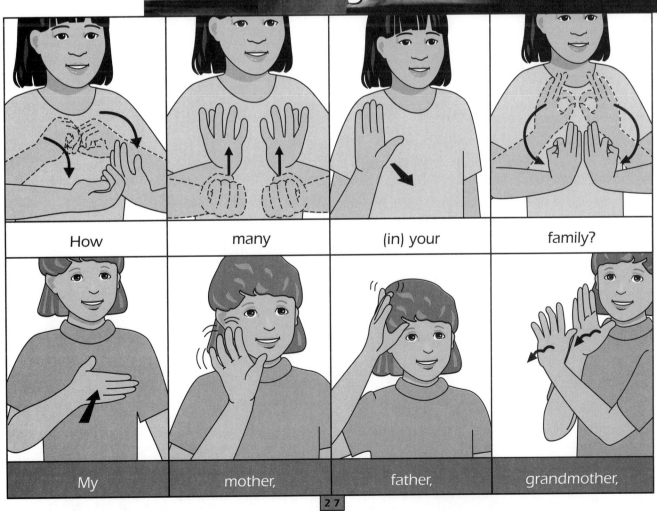

| How | many | (in) your | family? |
| My | mother, | father, | grandmother, |

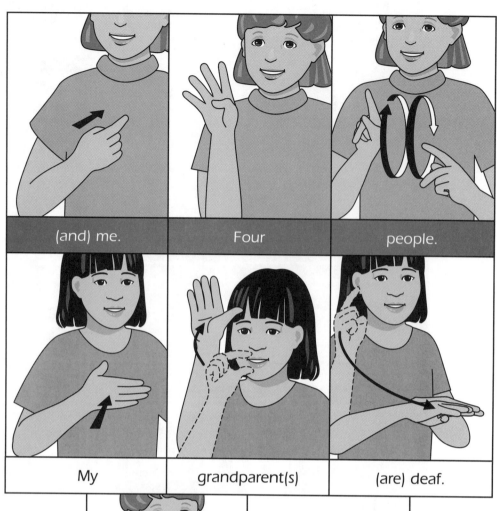

(and) me.	Four	people.
My	grandparent(s)	(are) deaf.

My	best
friend	(is) hard-of-hearing.

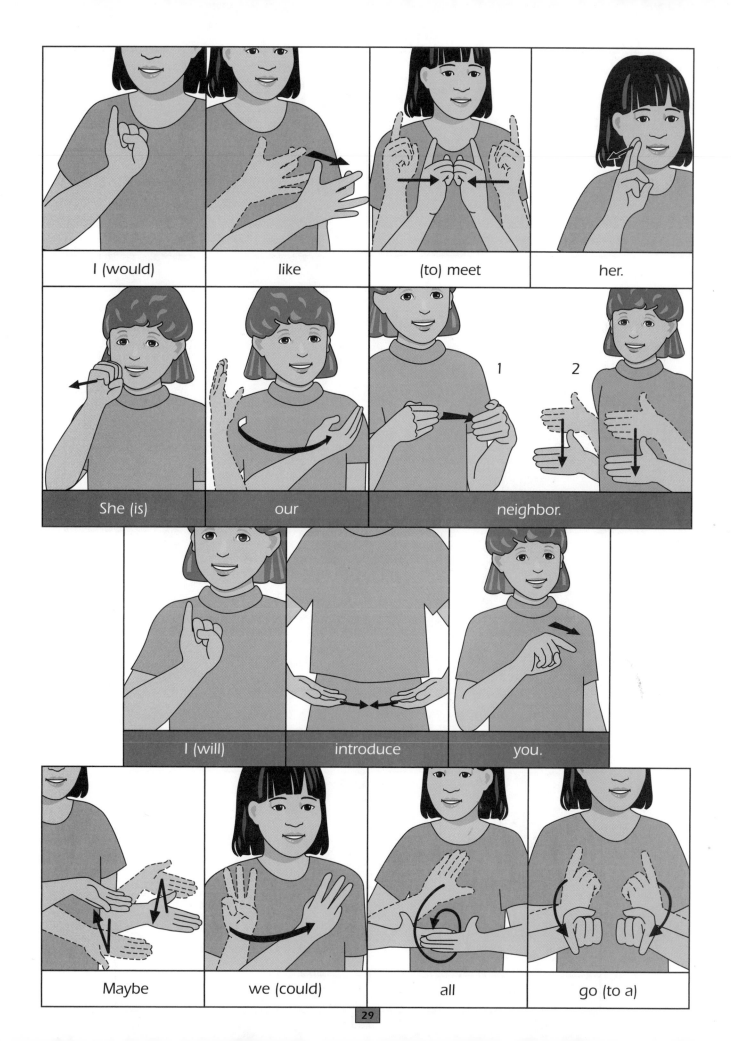

| I (would) | like | (to) meet | her. |

| She (is) | our | neighbor. | |

| I (will) | introduce | you. |

| Maybe | we (could) | all | go (to a) |

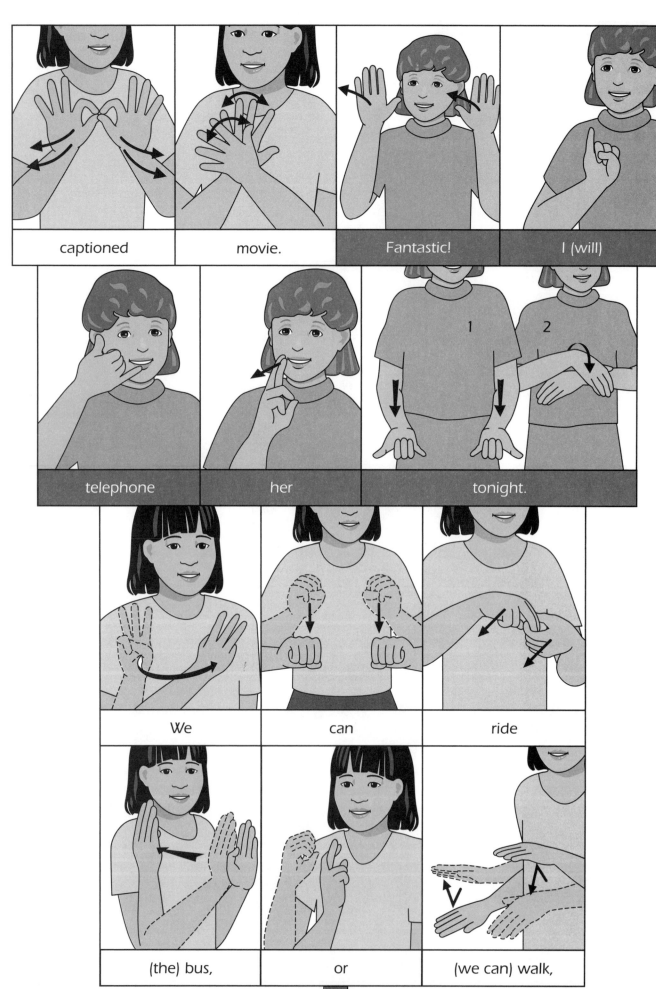

captioned	movie.	Fantastic!	I (will)

telephone	her	tonight.

We	can	ride

(the) bus,	or	(we can) walk,

30

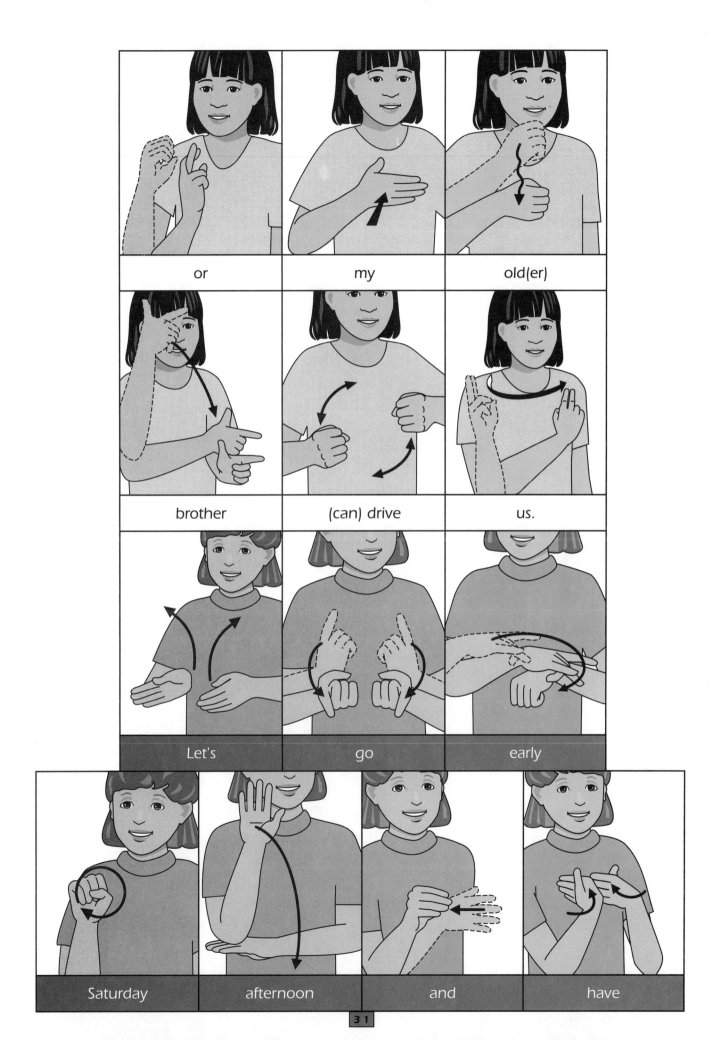

or	my	old(er)
brother	(can) drive	us.
Let's	go	early

| Saturday | afternoon | and | have |

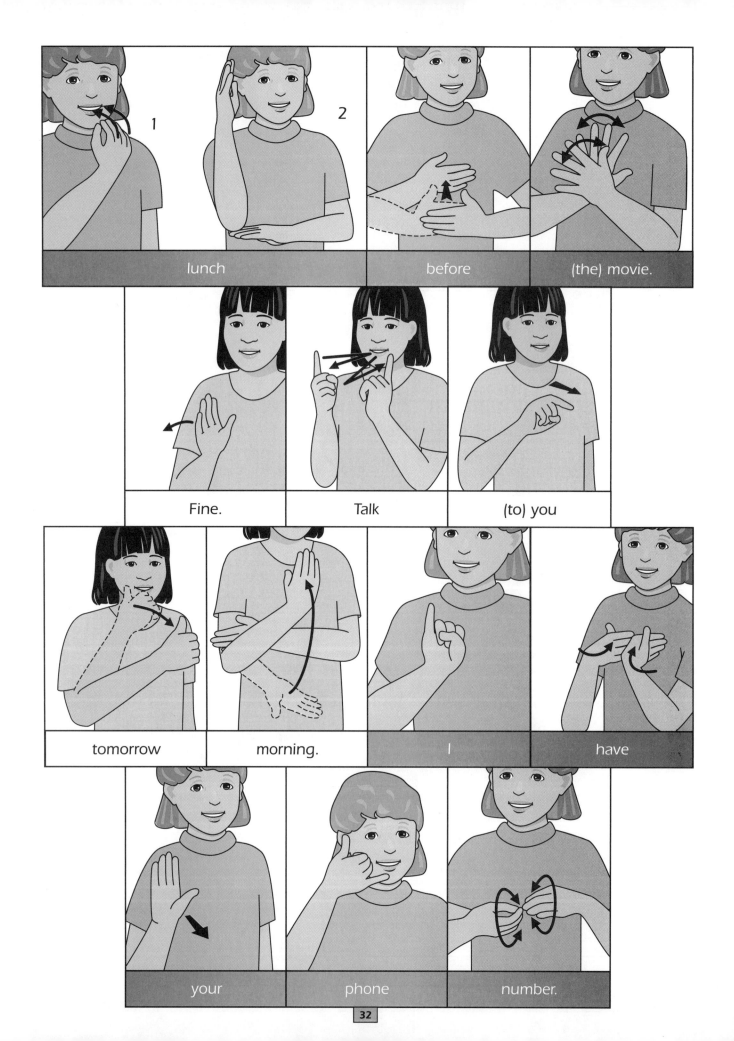

lunch | before | (the) movie.

Fine. | Talk | (to) you

tomorrow | morning. | I | have

your | phone | number.

Sequence:

Activities are not only for fun but also to introduce additional signs. In the groups to follow, at least one sign is labeled for you. Use your best reasoning to label the remaining signs in each group. Each group has a common theme. Arrange the signs in each group into a logical sequence. For instance, a logical sequence may be by size, time, length, or color.

1

fall (autumn)

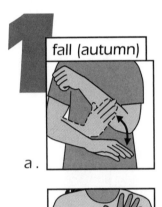
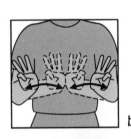

a.

b.

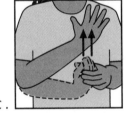
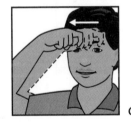

c.

d.

2

cow

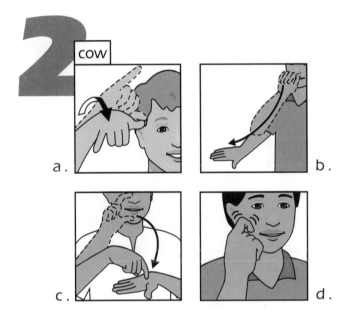

a.

b.

c.

d.

3

second

(quick)

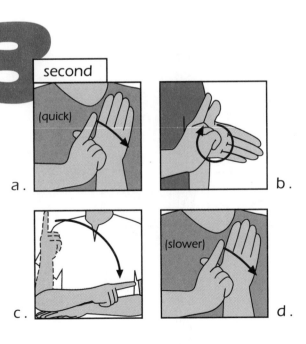

(slower)

a.

b.

c.

d.

4

tiny

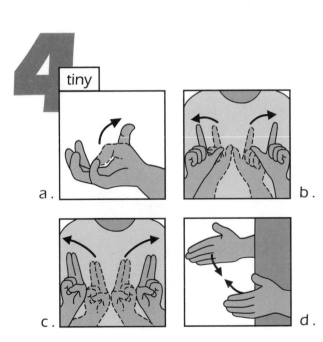

a.

b.

c.

d.

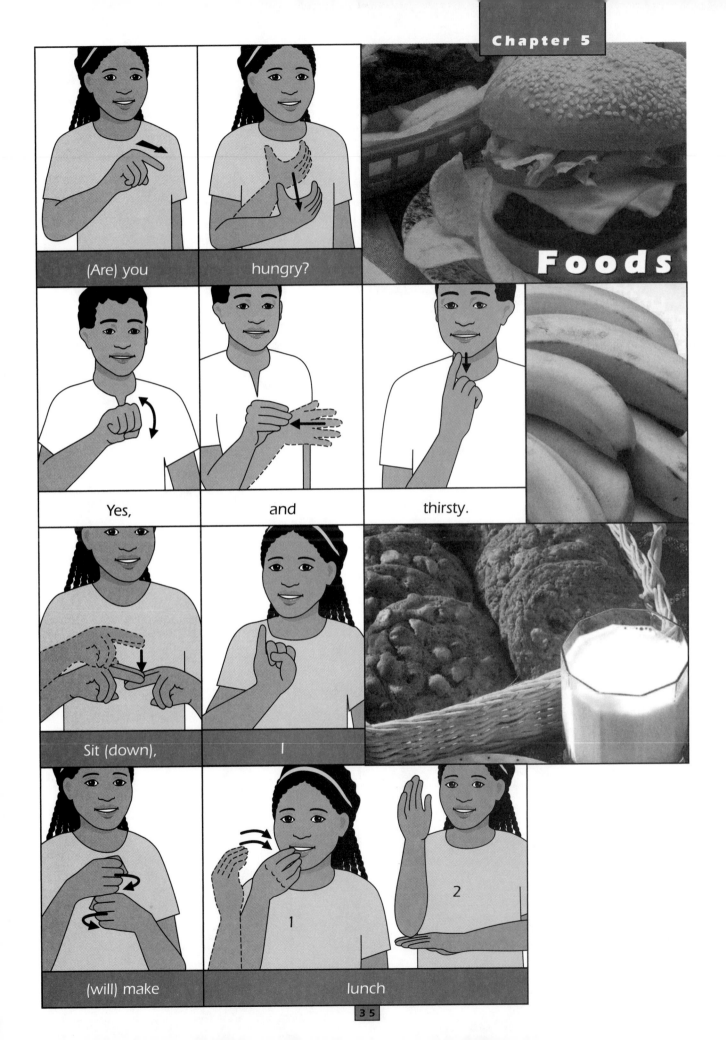

Chapter 5

(Are) you | hungry?

Foods

Yes, | and | thirsty.

Sit (down), | I

(will) make | lunch

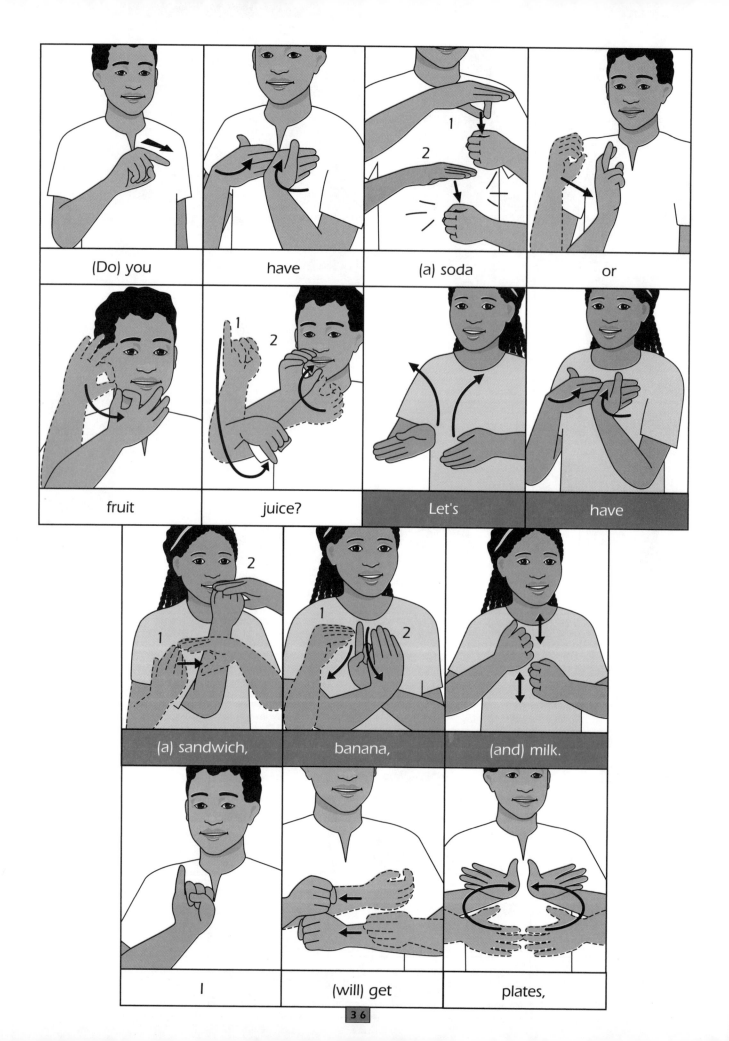

(Do) you	have	(a) soda	or
fruit	juice?	Let's	have

(a) sandwich,	banana,	(and) milk.

I	(will) get	plates,

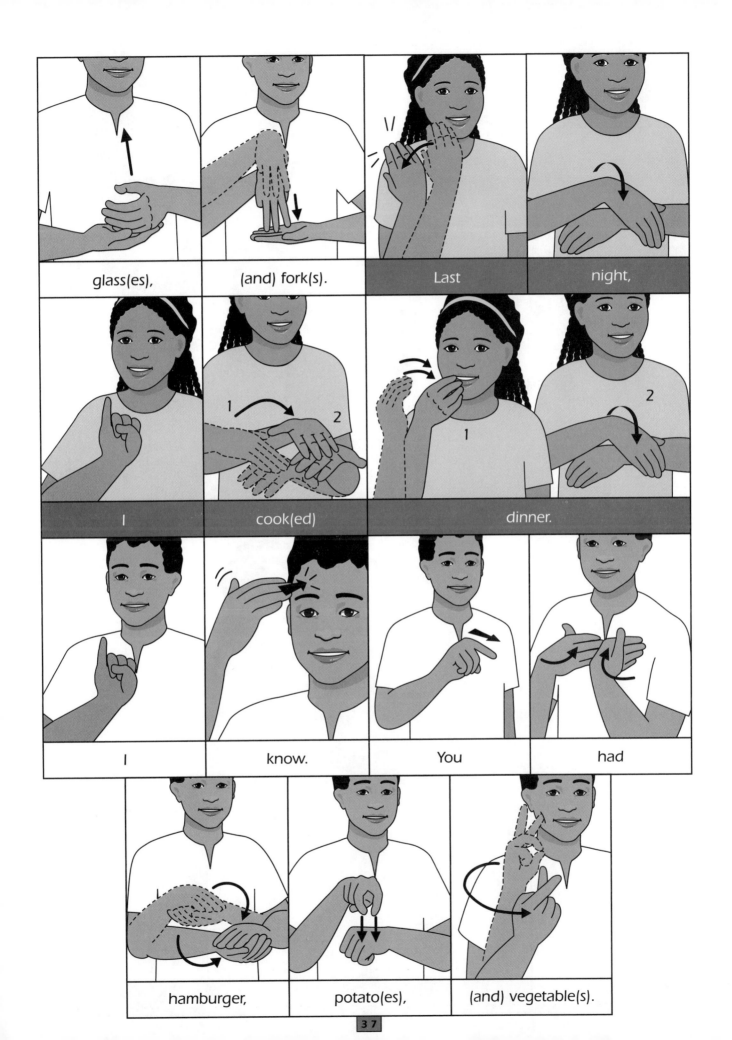

glass(es),	(and) fork(s).	Last	night,

| I | cook(ed) | dinner. | |

| I | know. | You | had |

hamburger,	potato(es),	(and) vegetable(s).

And   chocolate   cake   with

ice cream   for   dessert.

I   wonder,

(did) you   enjoy   your   meal?

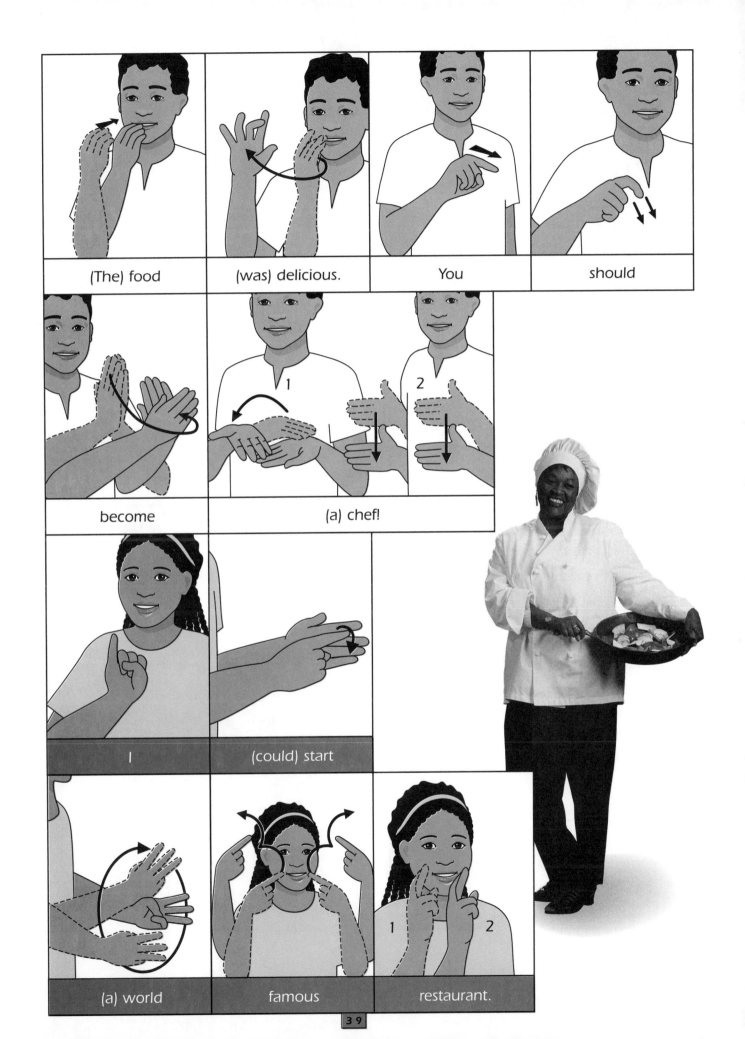

(The) food

(was) delicious.

You

should

become

(a) chef!

I

(could) start

(a) world

famous

restaurant.

Find the mismatch:

Three of the four signs in each row share something in common. One sign does not share that common feature. What do the three signs share in common? Which sign does not share the common feature?

New signs are labeled for you. Signs that have already been introduced to you are not labeled.

1.

2.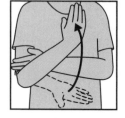

3.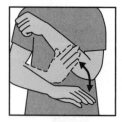

4.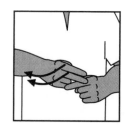

5.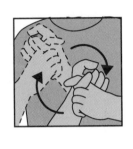

6.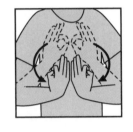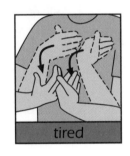

tired

7.

salad

cookie

8.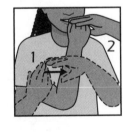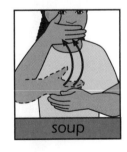

hot dog

soup

9.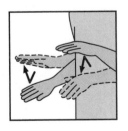

play

run

More mismatch:

Just like on the previous two pages, three of each of the examples share something in common:

What do they each have in common?

And which example does not follow the other three?

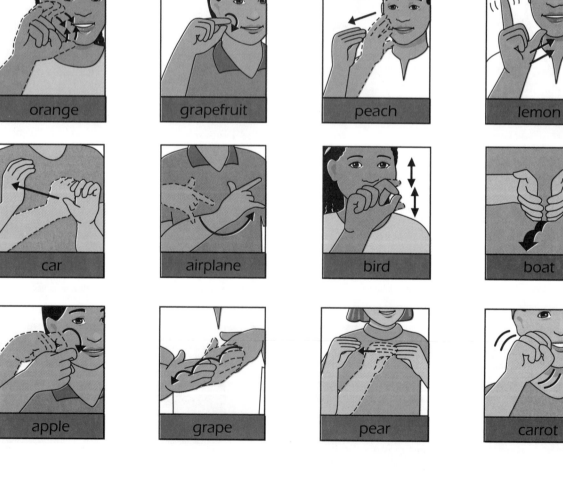

10. | meat | | | snack

11. | | candy | toast | bacon

12. | orange | grapefruit | peach | lemon

13. | car | airplane | bird | boat

14. | apple | grape | pear | carrot

Chapter 6

Health

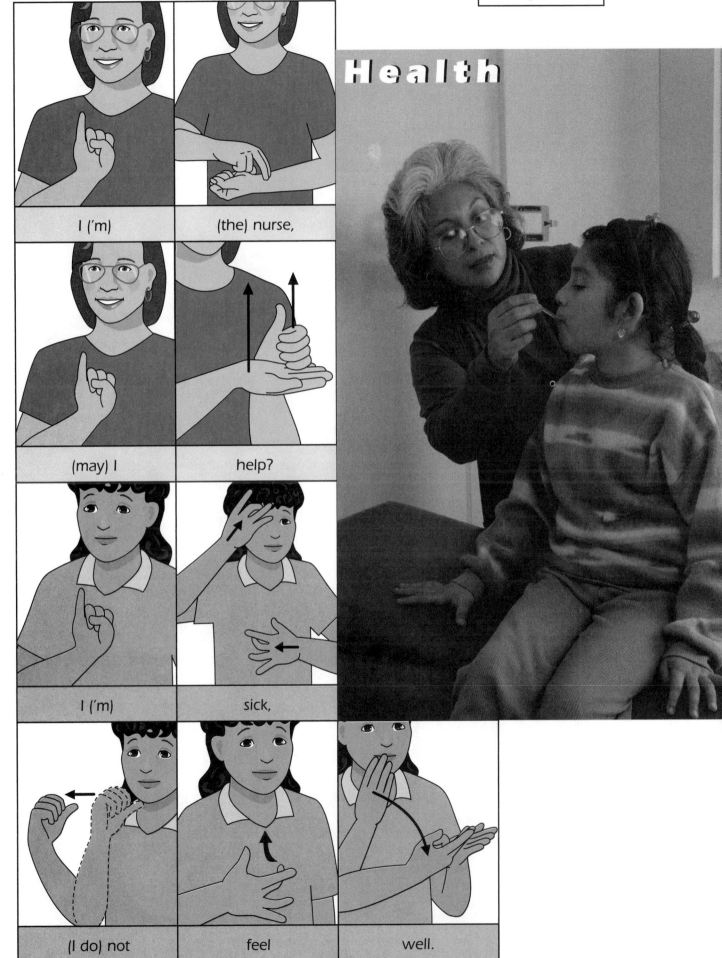

I ('m)

(the) nurse,

(may) I

help?

I ('m)

sick,

(I do) not

feel

well.

Stomachache, | headache, | what?

My | nose, | ear(s), | (and) throat

hurt. | Let | me | examine

you. | Lie (down) | please.

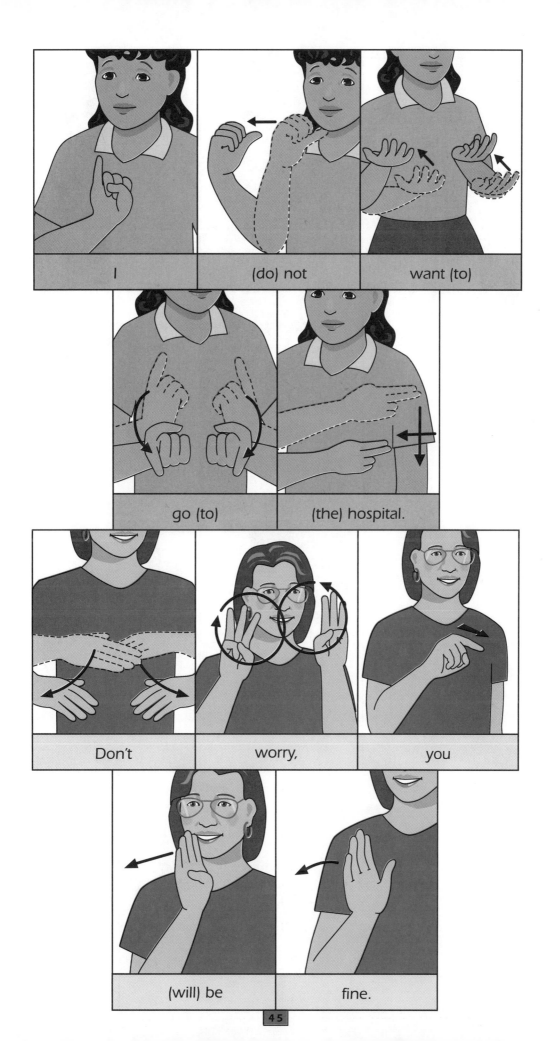

I	(do) not	want (to)

go (to)	(the) hospital.

Don't	worry,	you

(will) be	fine.

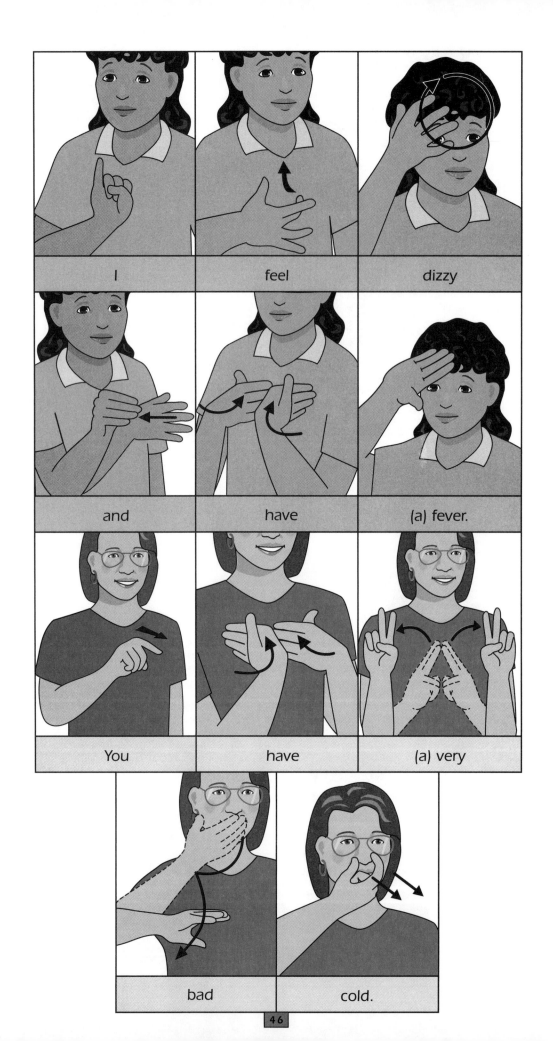

I	feel	dizzy
and	have	(a) fever.
You	have	(a) very

| bad | cold. |

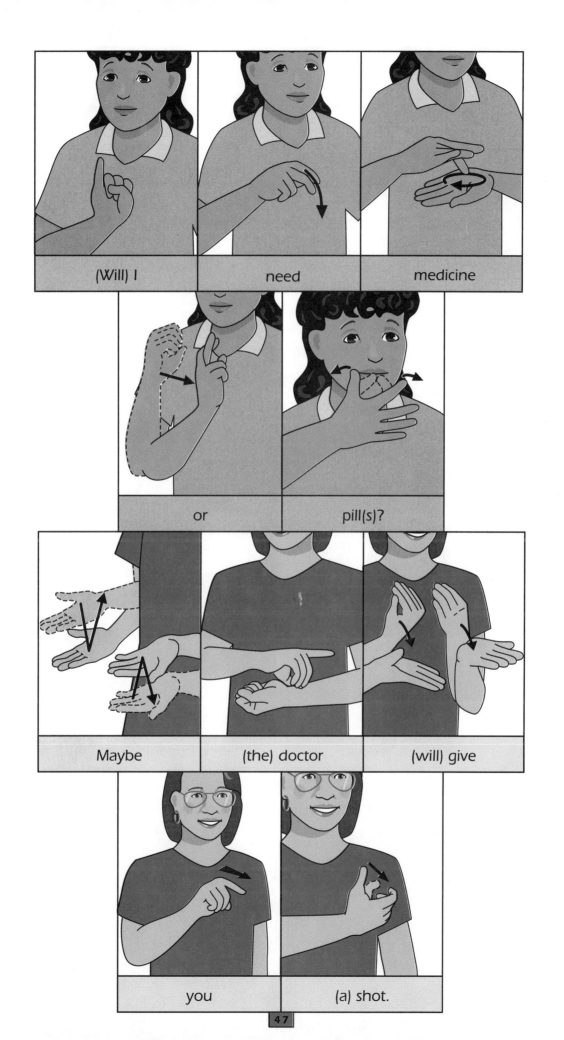

(Will) I   need   medicine

or   pill(s)?

Maybe   (the) doctor   (will) give

you   (a) shot.

But,	(will) I	feel

better	tomorrow?

Yes.	Ask (for)	(an) appointment	(to) return

(in) one	week.	OK.	Thanks.

Part 1:

Many times you can guess what a sign means without being told. First, can you create your own sign for these words? Second, match the words with the signs. How close is the sign you created to the sign given?

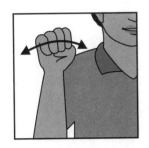

A.

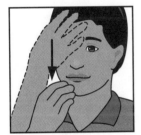

B.

C.

D.

E.

1. break
   (as in a fracture)

2. nauseous,
   upset stomach

3. throw up, vomit

4. emergency

5. look, watch, see

6. bath, bathe, wash

7. bed or sleep

8. cut

9. hearing aid

10. lie down

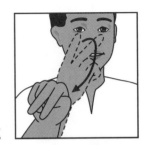

F.

G.

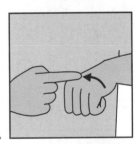

H.

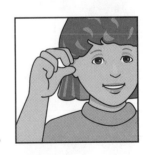

I.

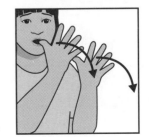

J.

Part 2:

What body parts do these pictures suggest?

Match the pictures with the signs:
    Head, face, neck, eye, teeth, hand, feet, leg, body, heart

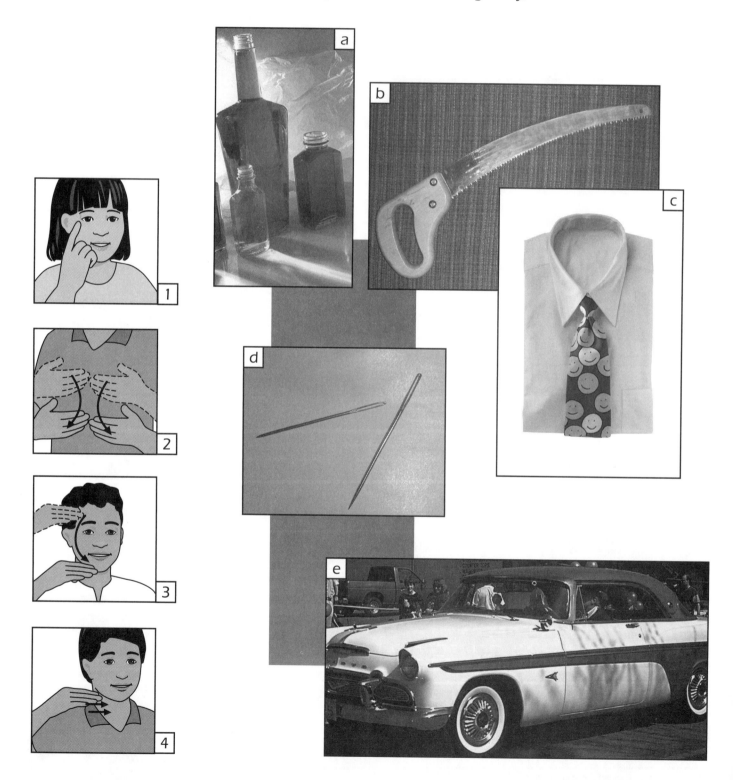

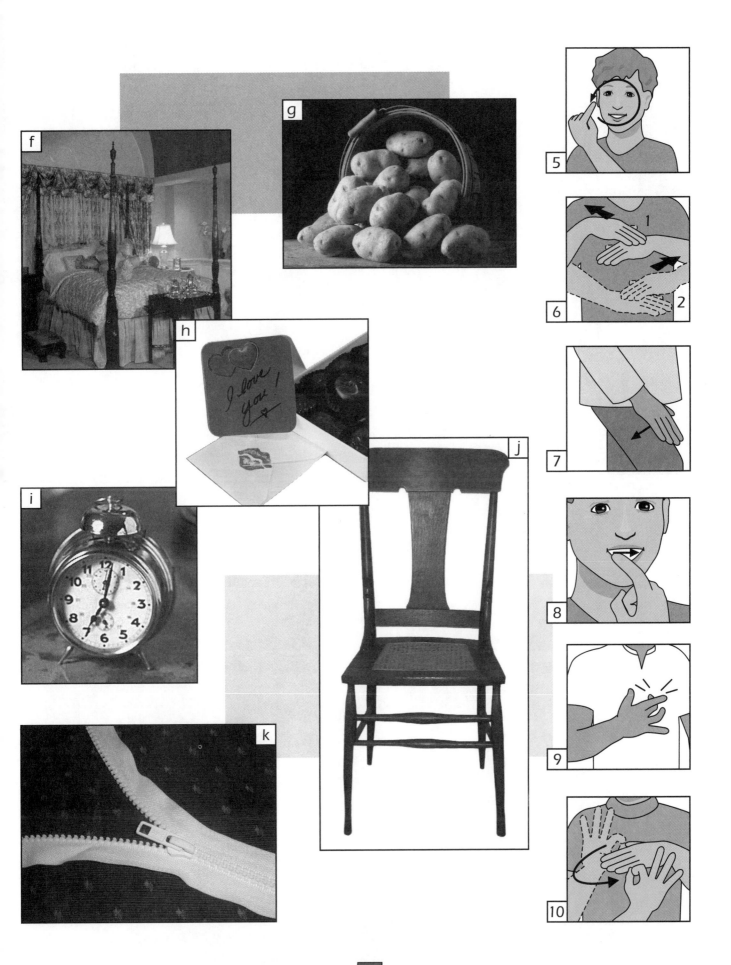

Chapter 7

Clothes and Shopping

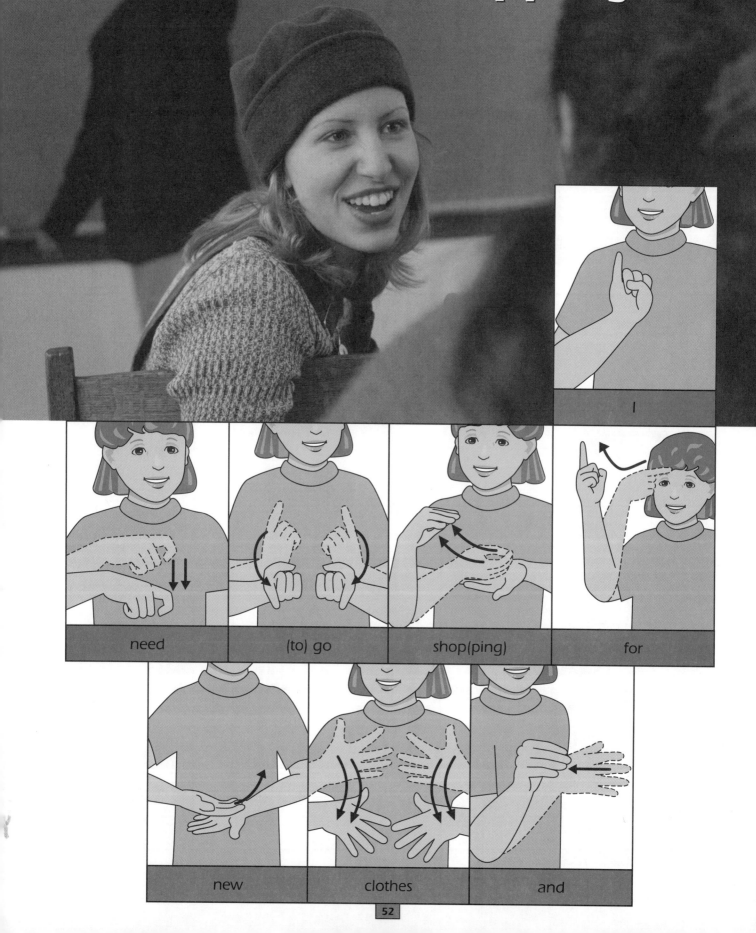

I

need   (to) go   shop(ping)   for

new   clothes   and

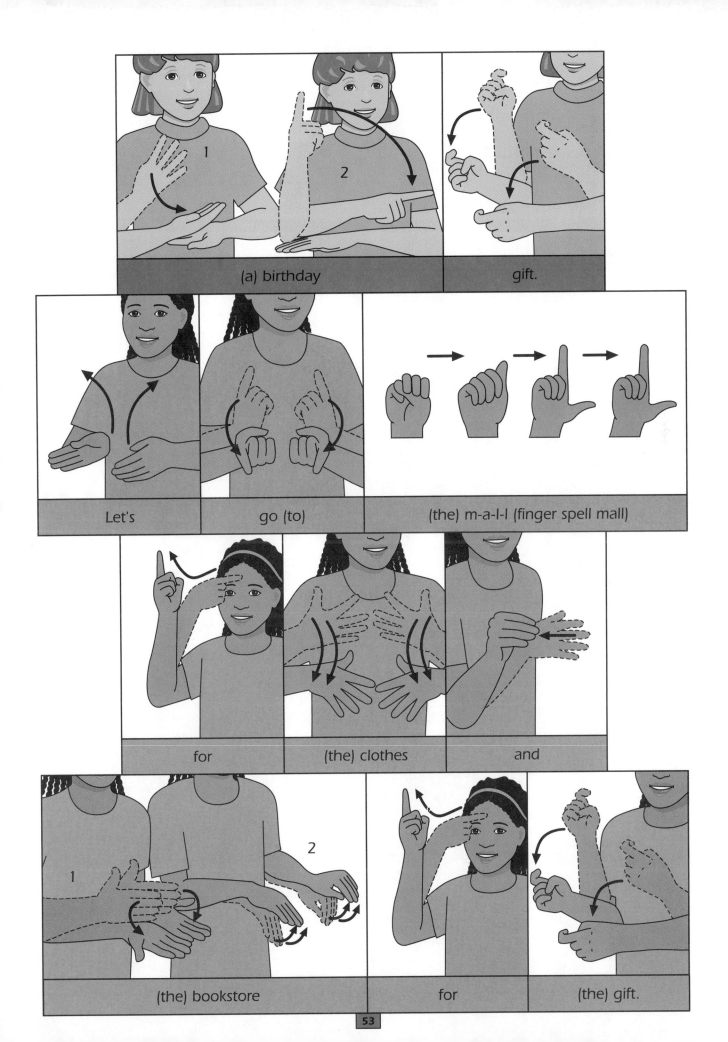

(a) birthday

gift.

Let's

go (to)

(the) m-a-l-l (finger spell mall)

for

(the) clothes

and

(the) bookstore

for

(the) gift.

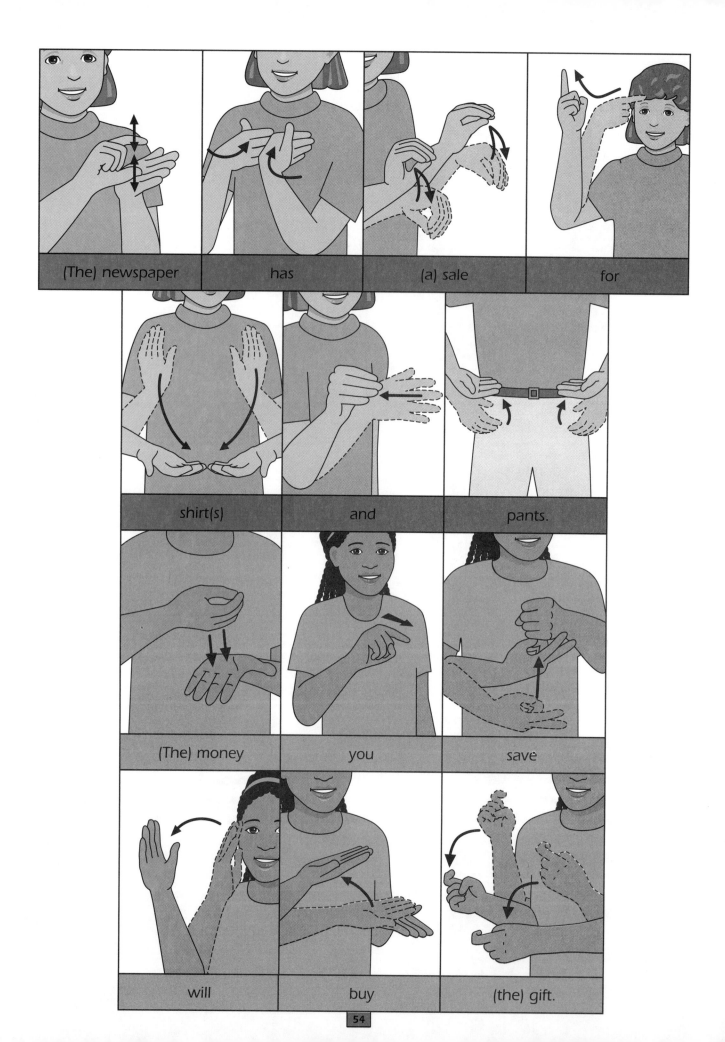

(The) newspaper	has	(a) sale	for

shirt(s)	and	pants.

(The) money	you	save

will	buy	(the) gift.

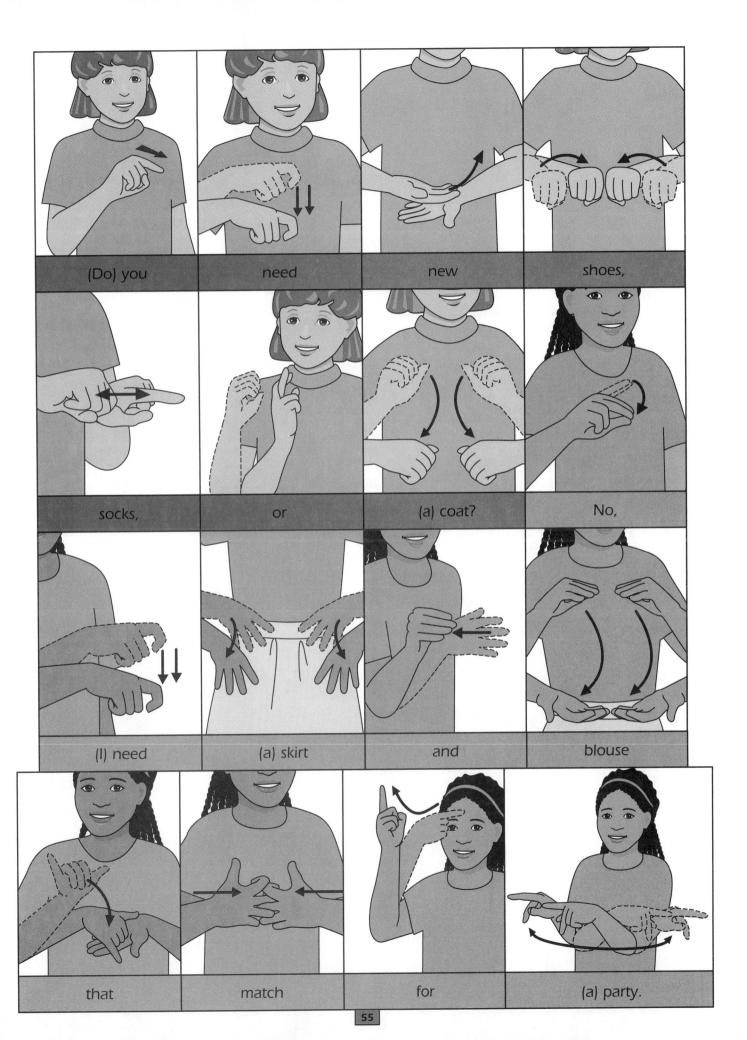

(Do) you	need	new	shoes,
socks,	or	(a) coat?	No,
(I) need	(a) skirt	and	blouse
that	match	for	(a) party.

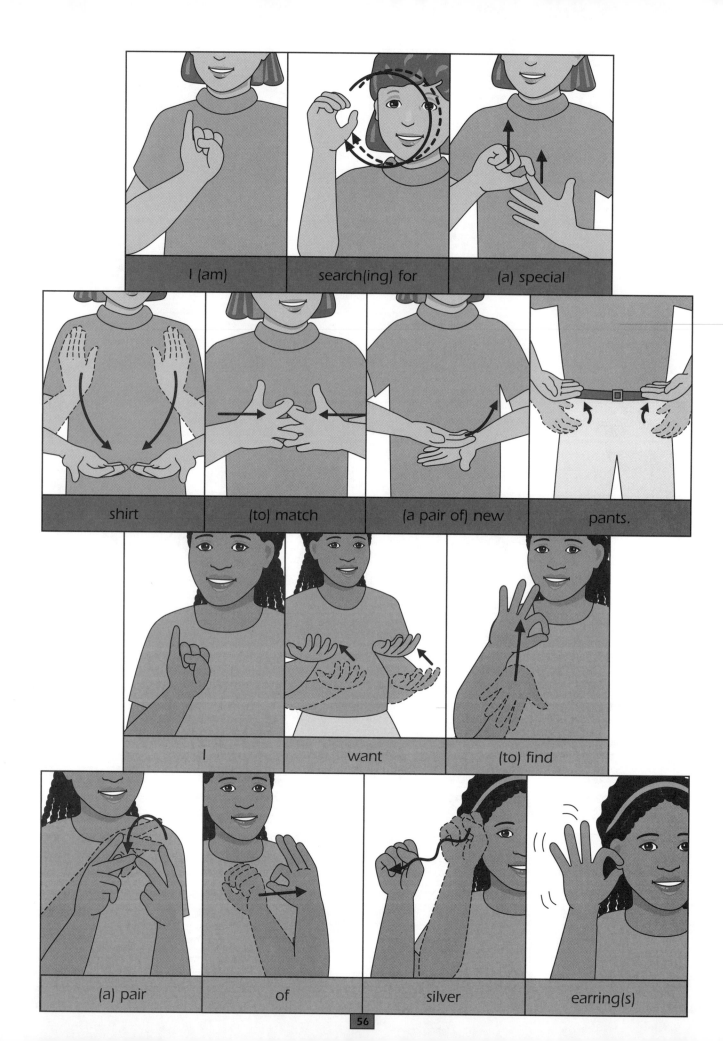

I (am)	search(ing) for	(a) special

shirt	(to) match	(a pair of) new	pants.

I	want	(to) find

(a) pair	of	silver	earring(s)

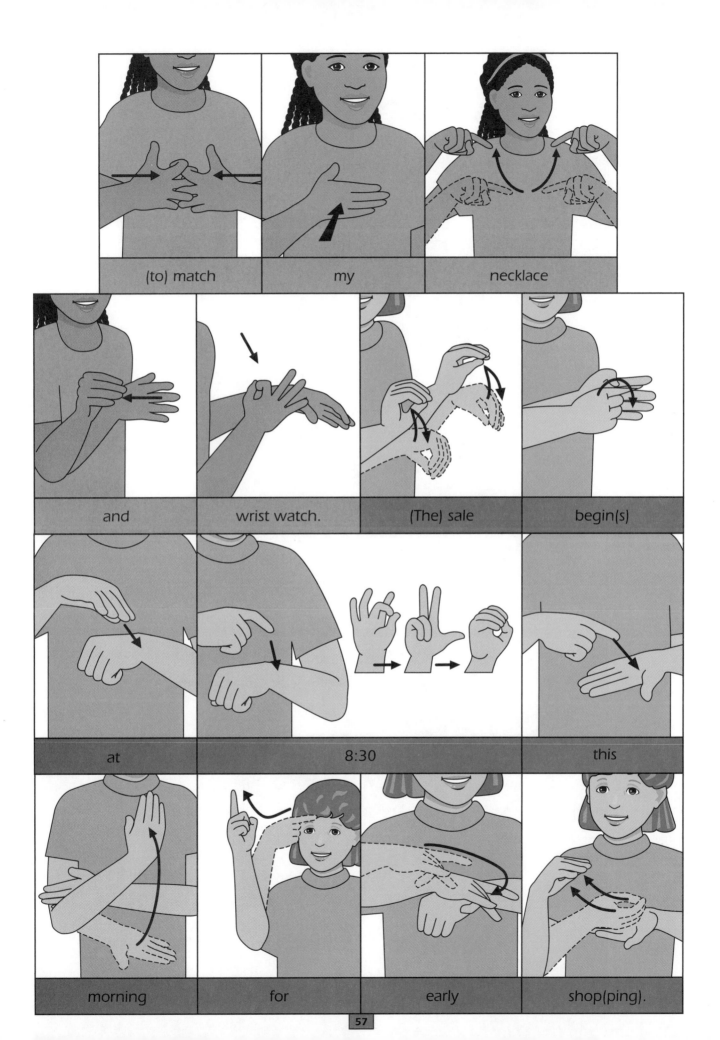

(to) match | my | necklace

and | wrist watch. | (The) sale | begin(s)

at | 8:30 | this

morning | for | early | shop(ping).

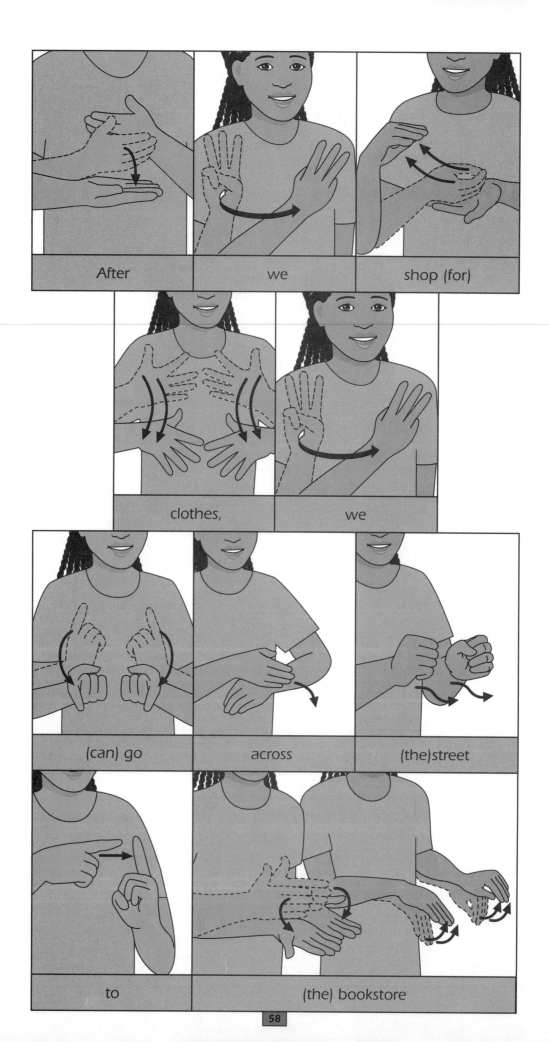

After   we   shop (for)

clothes,   we

(can) go   across   (the) street

to   (the) bookstore

My uncle just

return(ed) from (a) wonderful

trip to Italy.

Give him

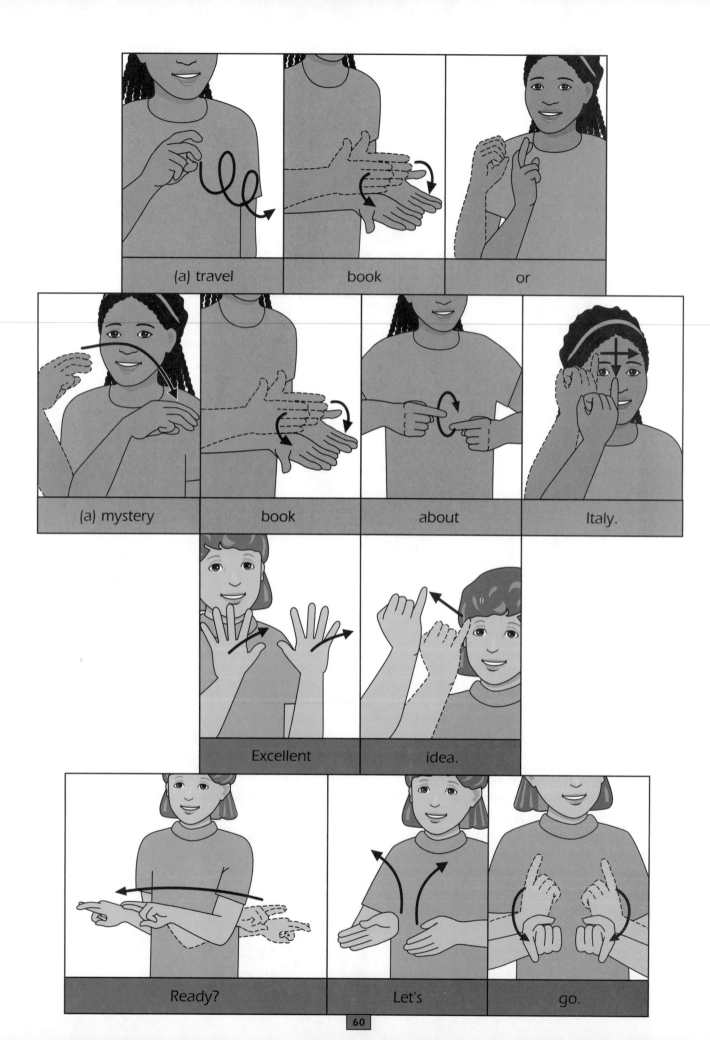

(a) travel   book   or

(a) mystery   book   about   Italy.

Excellent   idea.

Ready?   Let's   go.

Go together:

Pair two signs that go together. For example #3 (sell) goes with #5 (buy). You will note that the new signs have been labeled. Signs that you have already learned are not labeled.

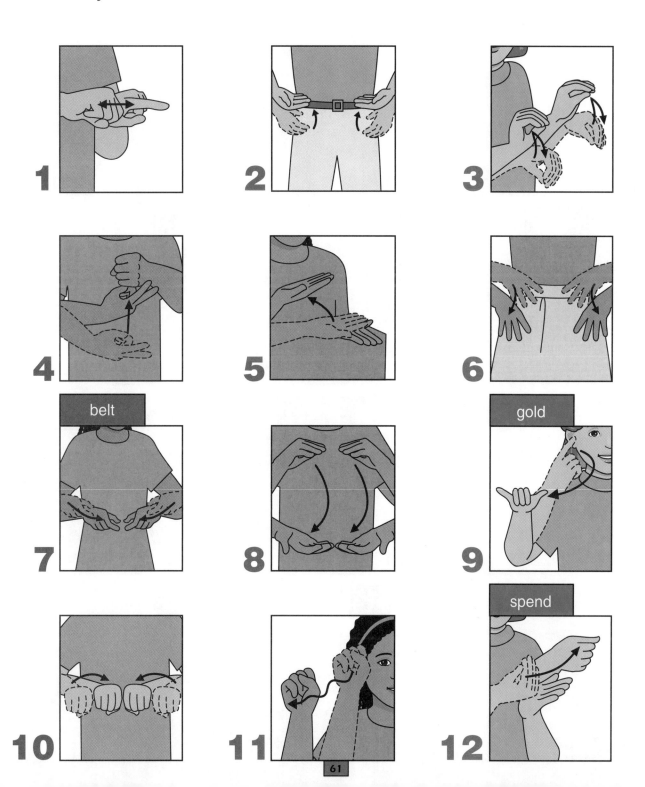

1

2

3

4

5

6

belt

7

8

gold

9

10

11

spend

12

More Go together:

Pair two signs that go together. The new signs have been labeled.
Remember, signs that you have already learned are not labeled.

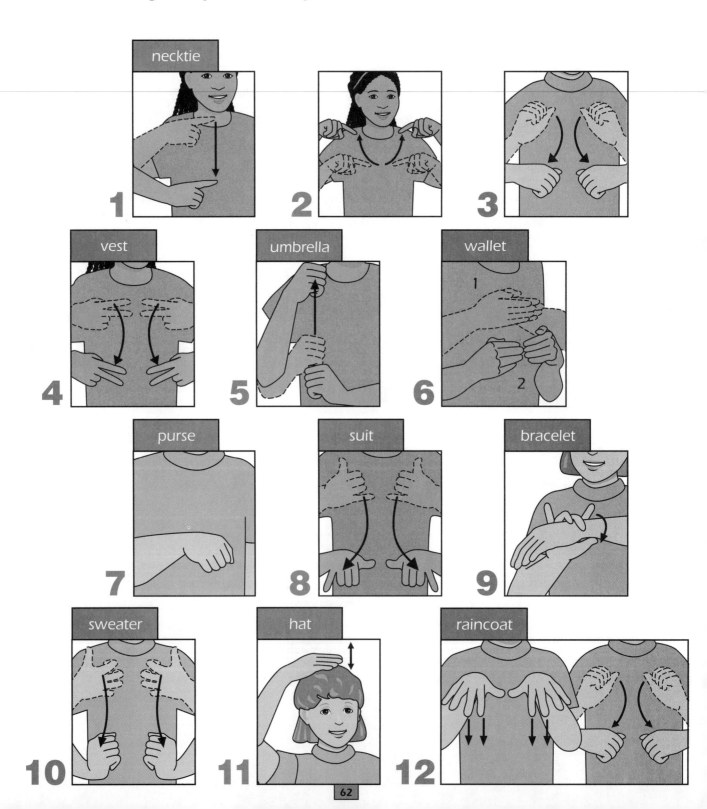

Chapter 8

Pets, Animals & Colors

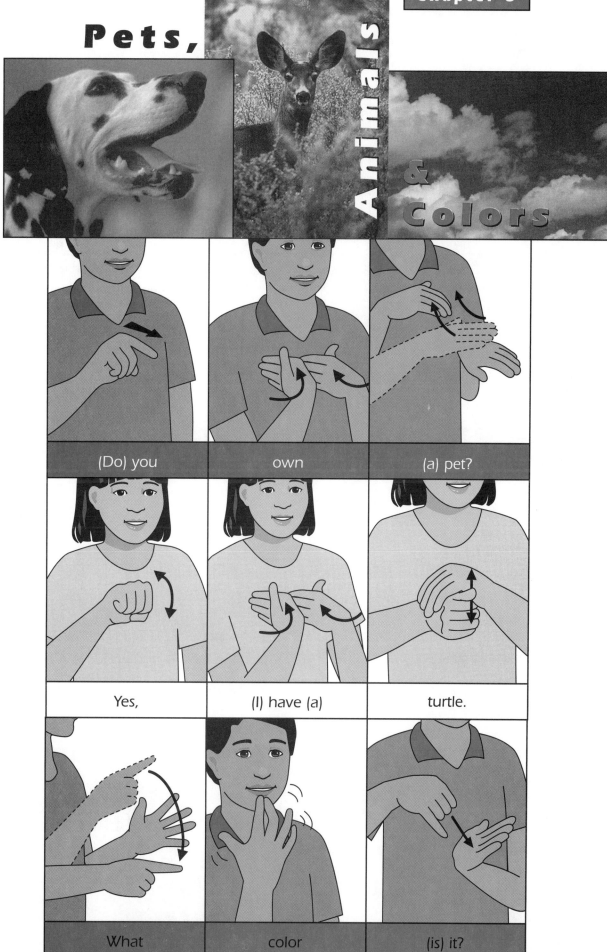

(Do) you	own	(a) pet?
Yes,	(I) have (a)	turtle.
What	color	(is) it?

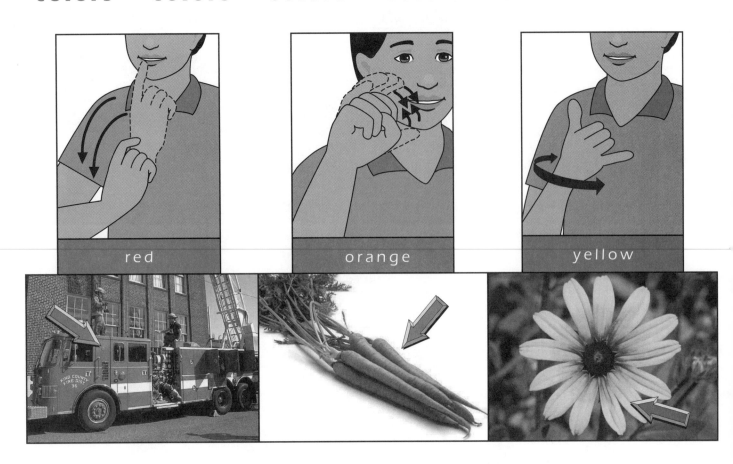

red

orange

yellow

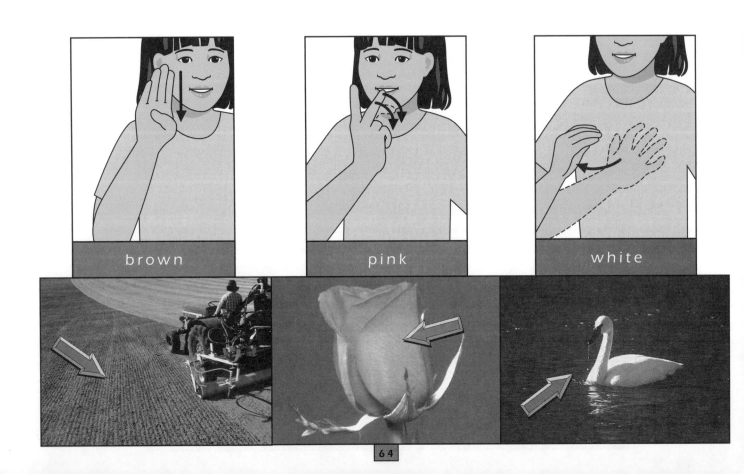

brown

pink

white

green

blue

purple

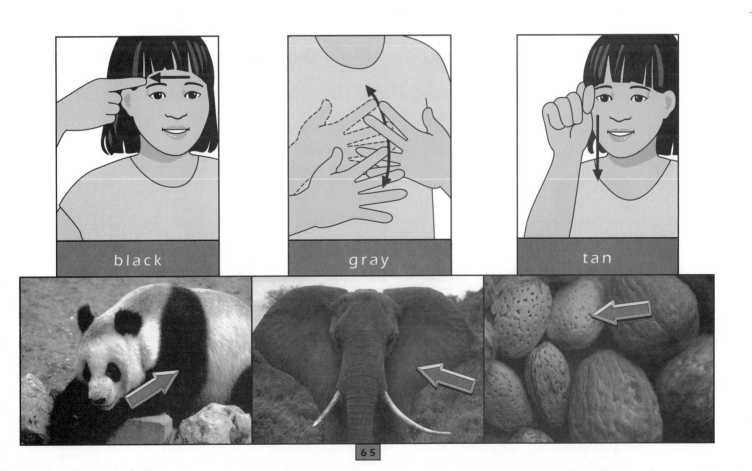

black

gray

tan

chicken

duck

sheep

cow

horse

goat

lion

deer

zebra

pig

fish

mouse

bear

cat

dog

rabbit

tiger

snake

Animal Signs You Can Guess:

Can you guess these animal signs? Like so many signs, these animal signs are a giveaway!

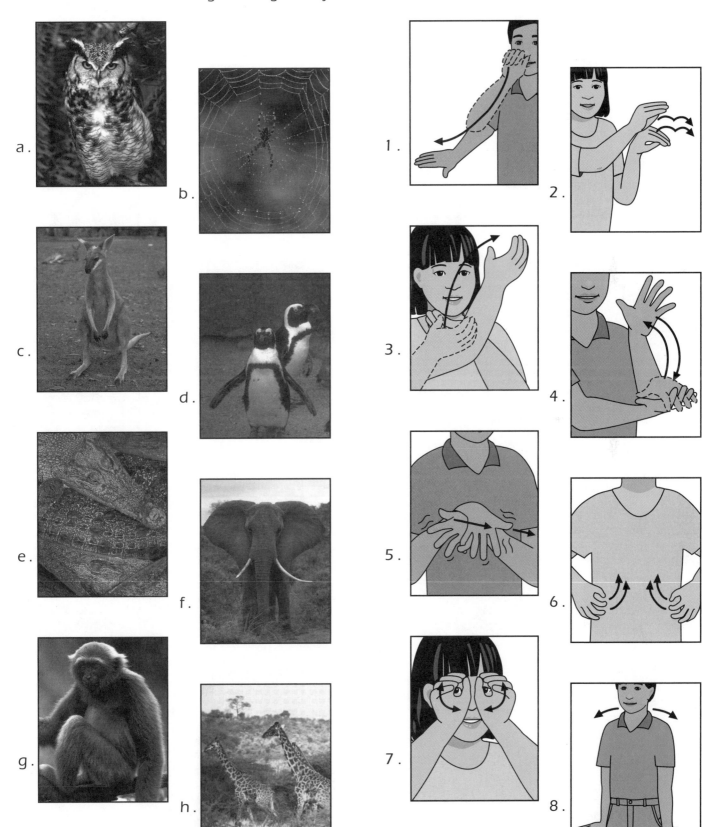

a.

b.

c.

d.

e.

f.

g.

h.

1.

2.

3.

4.

5.

6.

7.

8.

Animal Babies:

You know the signs for the parent animal, can you tell what the sign is for the baby?

a.

b.

c.

d.

e.

f.

g.

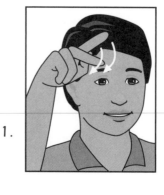

1.

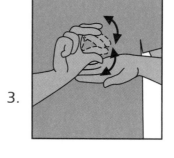

3.

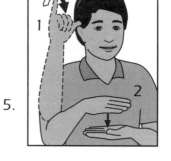

5.

7.

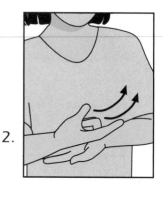

2.

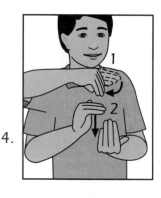

4.

6.

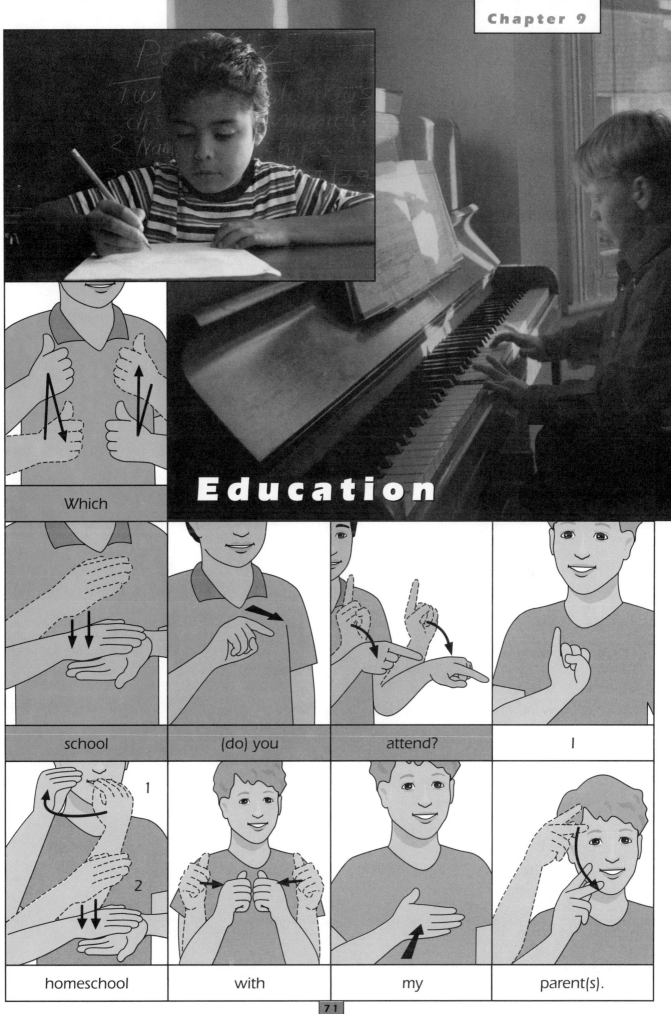

Chapter 9

Education

Which			
school	(do) you	attend?	I
homeschool	with	my	parent(s).

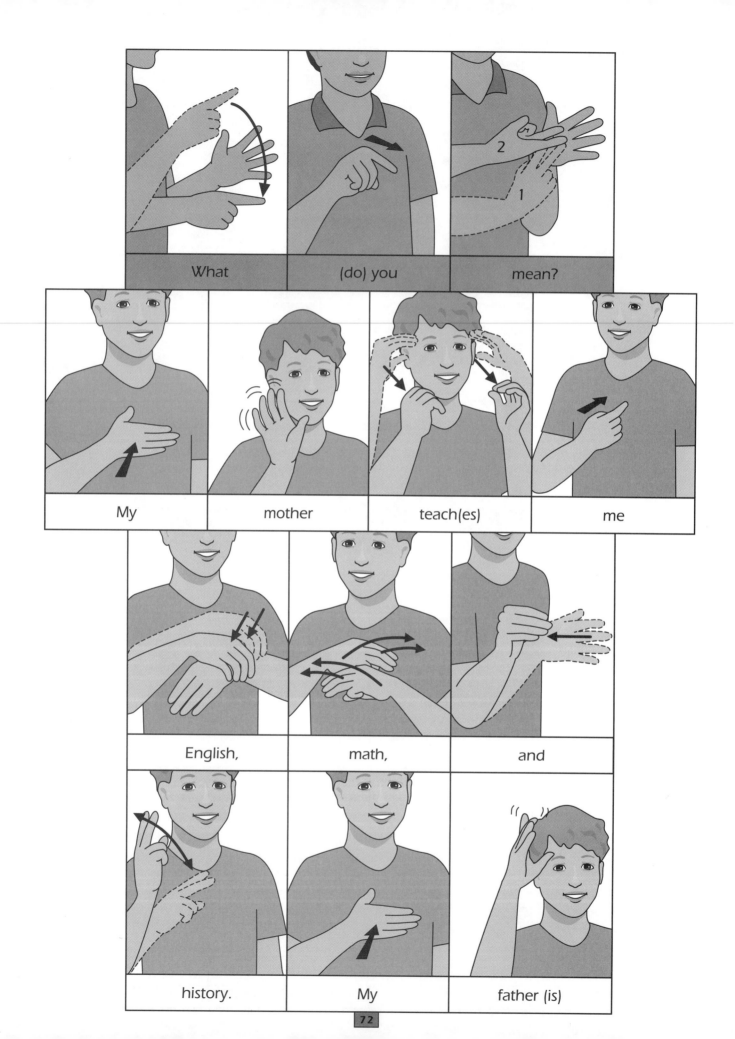

| What | (do) you | mean? |

| My | mother | teach(es) | me |

| English, | math, | and |

| history. | My | father (is) |

my	science,	music,

and	sign language	teacher (teach-person).

I	study	(the) same

subject(s)	at	school.

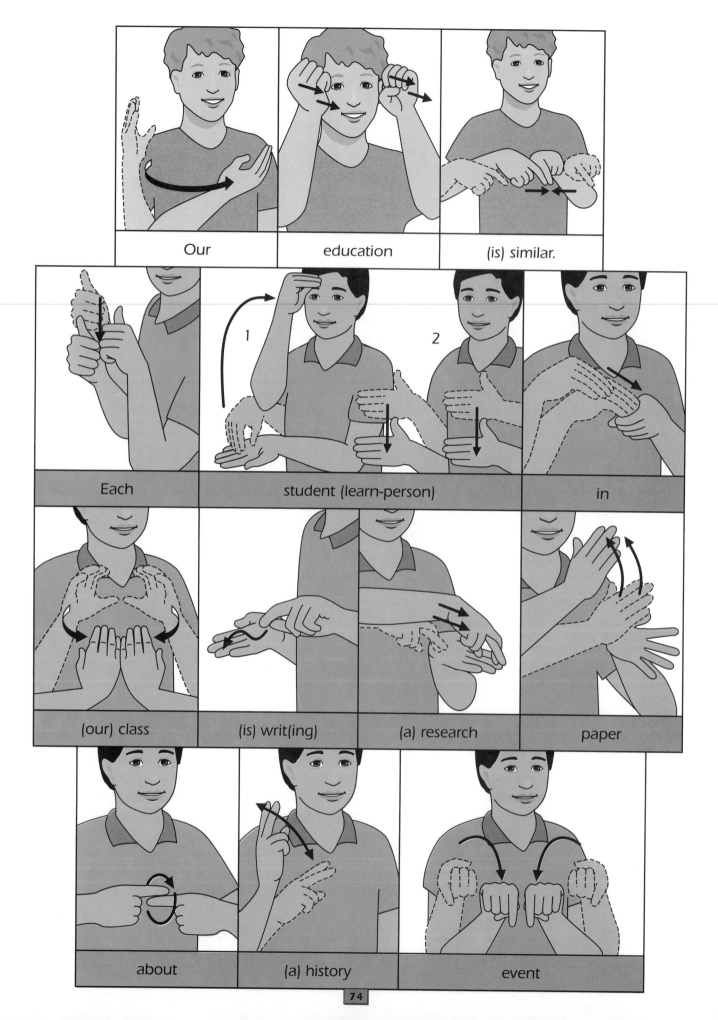

Our education (is) similar.

Each student (learn-person) in

(our) class (is) writ(ing) (a) research paper

about (a) history event

74

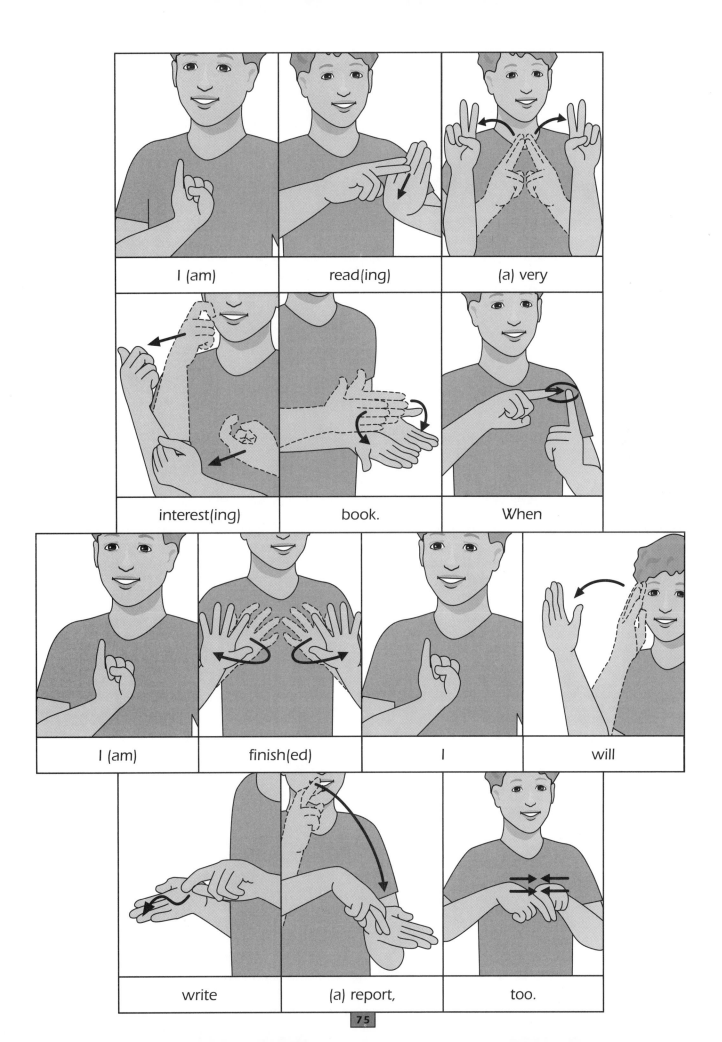

I (am)	read(ing)	(a) very
interest(ing)	book.	When

I (am)	finish(ed)	I	will

write	(a) report,	too.

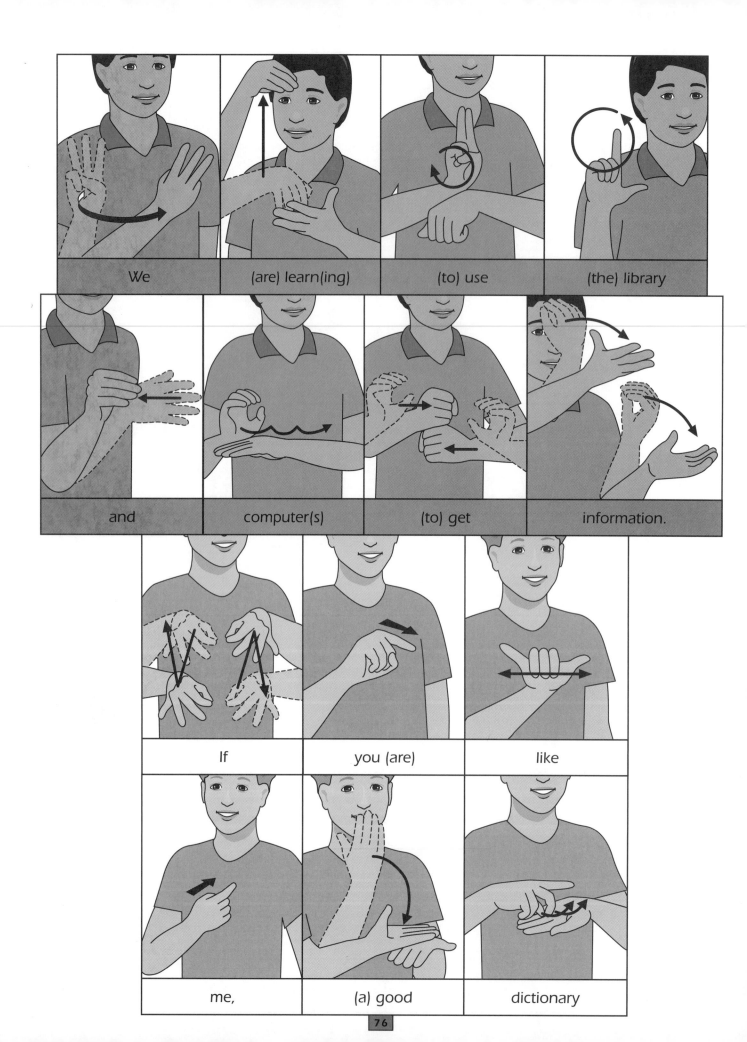

We	(are) learn(ing)	(to) use	(the) library

and	computer(s)	(to) get	information.

If	you (are)	like

me,	(a) good	dictionary

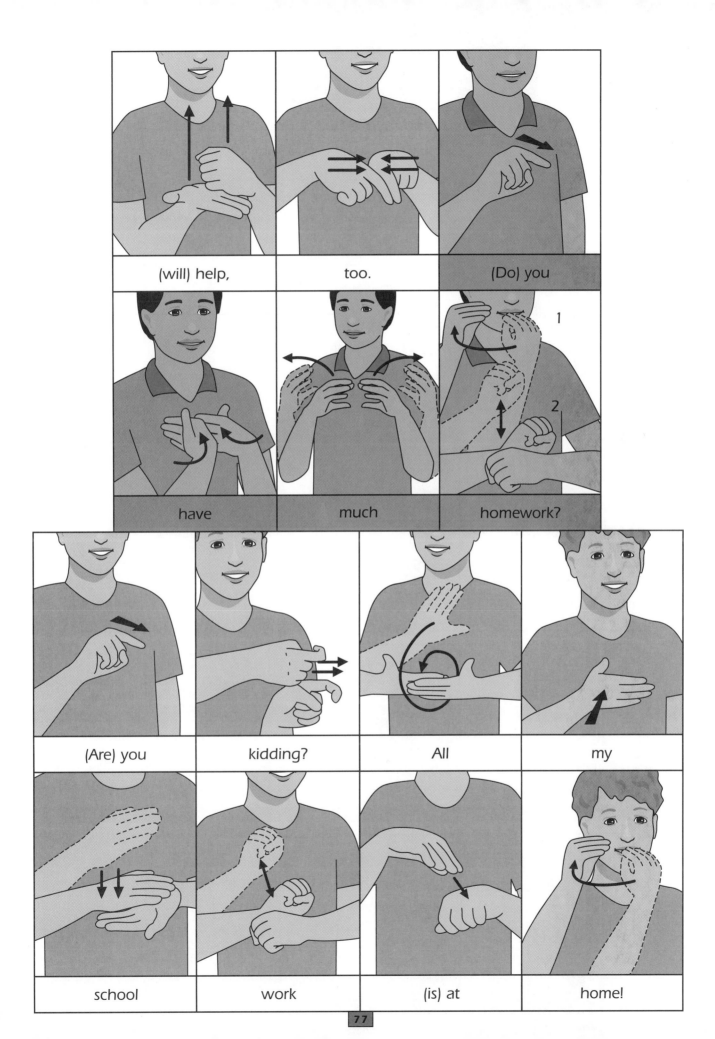

(will) help,	too.	(Do) you
have	much	homework?

(Are) you	kidding?	All	my
school	work	(is) at	home!

Analogies:

Complete each comparison by using one of the signs from the Answer Choices on the next page. The signs you already know are not labeled. New signs to learn have labels.

1 | baseball | is to | throw | as | football | is to what?

2 | nose | is to | smell | as | finger | is to what?

3 | grass | is to | green | as | sky | is to what?

4 | fish | is to | swim | as | person | is to what?

5 | hotdog | is to | eat | as | milk | is to what?

6 | monkey | is to | tree | as | hippo | is to what?

7 | ? | is to | ? | as | hand | is to what?

Answers Choices

A. touch

B. drink

C. water

D. ?

E. ?

F. glove

G. kick

This page has more comparison sentences similar to those on the previous pages. Complete each comparison by using one of the Answer Choices. Some signs you already know. As before, new signs are labeled.

8	tree	is to	forest	as	water	is to what?
9	one	is to	two	as	?	is to what?
10	?	is to	?	as	?	is to what?
11	winter	is to	snow	as	summer	is to what?

12   ?   is to   ?   as   apple   is to what?

13   cool   is to   ?   as   warm   is to what?

14   heavy   is to   light   as   large   is to what?

Answer Choices

A. ?

B. small

C. hot

D. lake

E. sun

F. ?

G. ?

Chapter 10

Sports

(Do) you	have	(a) favorite	sport?

I	like	(to) play	football

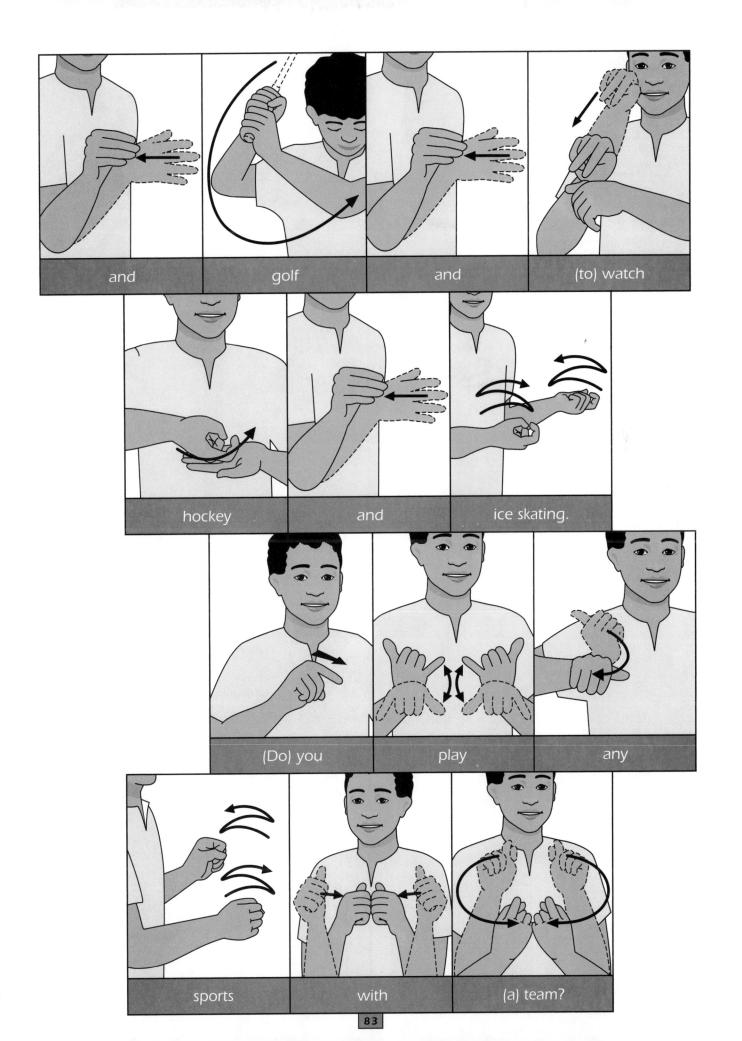

and golf and (to) watch

hockey and ice skating.

(Do) you play any

sports with (a) team?

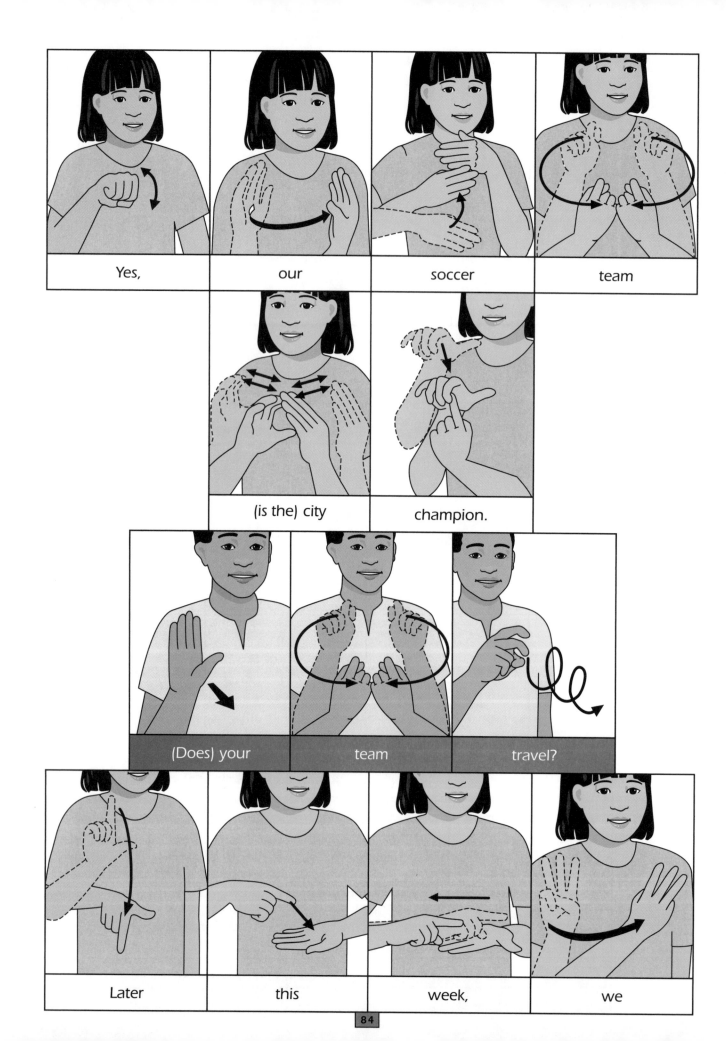

| Yes, | our | soccer | team |

| (is the) city | champion. |

(Does) your   team   travel?

| Later | this | week, | we |

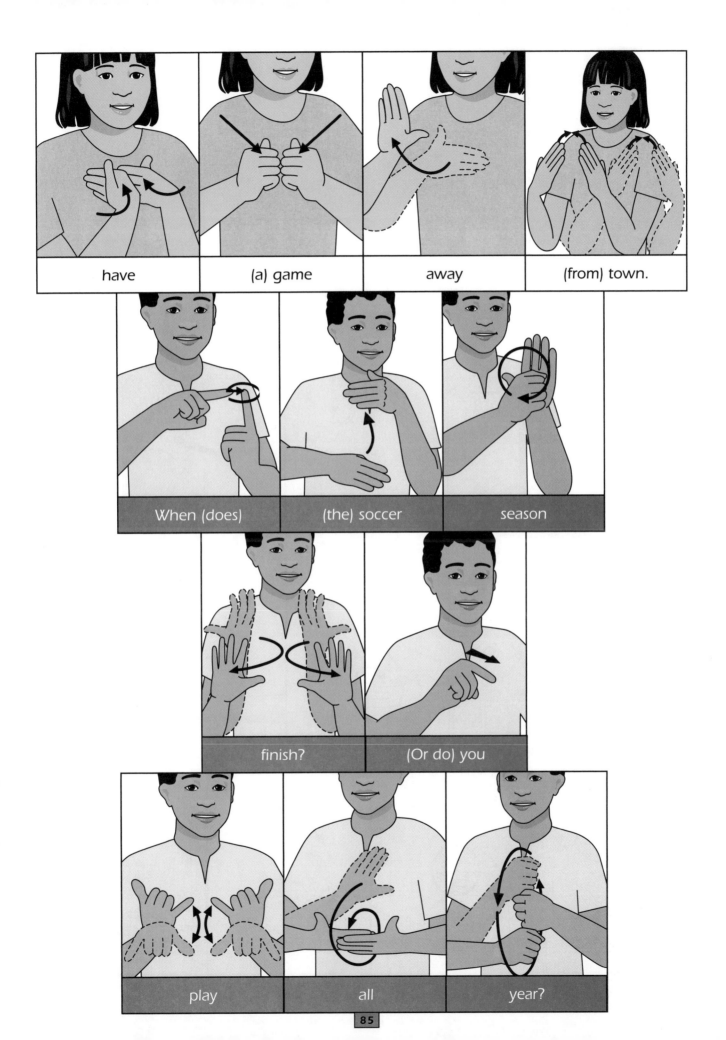

have   (a) game   away   (from) town.

When (does)   (the) soccer   season

finish?   (Or do) you

play   all   year?

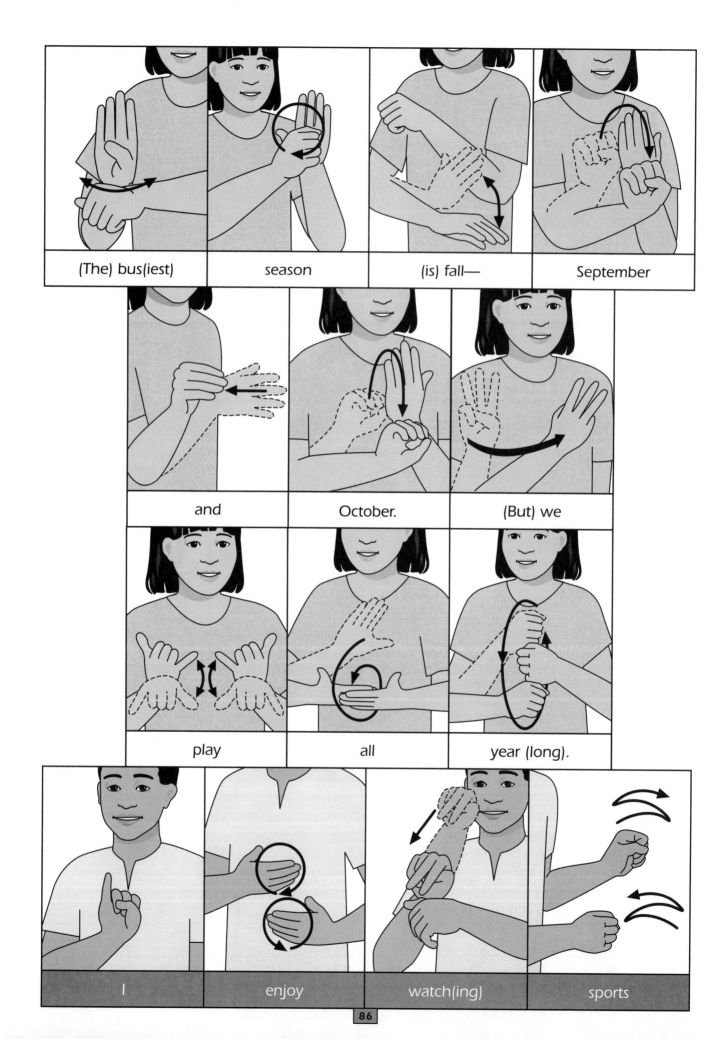

(The) bus(iest)	season	(is) fall—	September

and	October.	(But) we

play	all	year (long).

I	enjoy	watch(ing)	sports

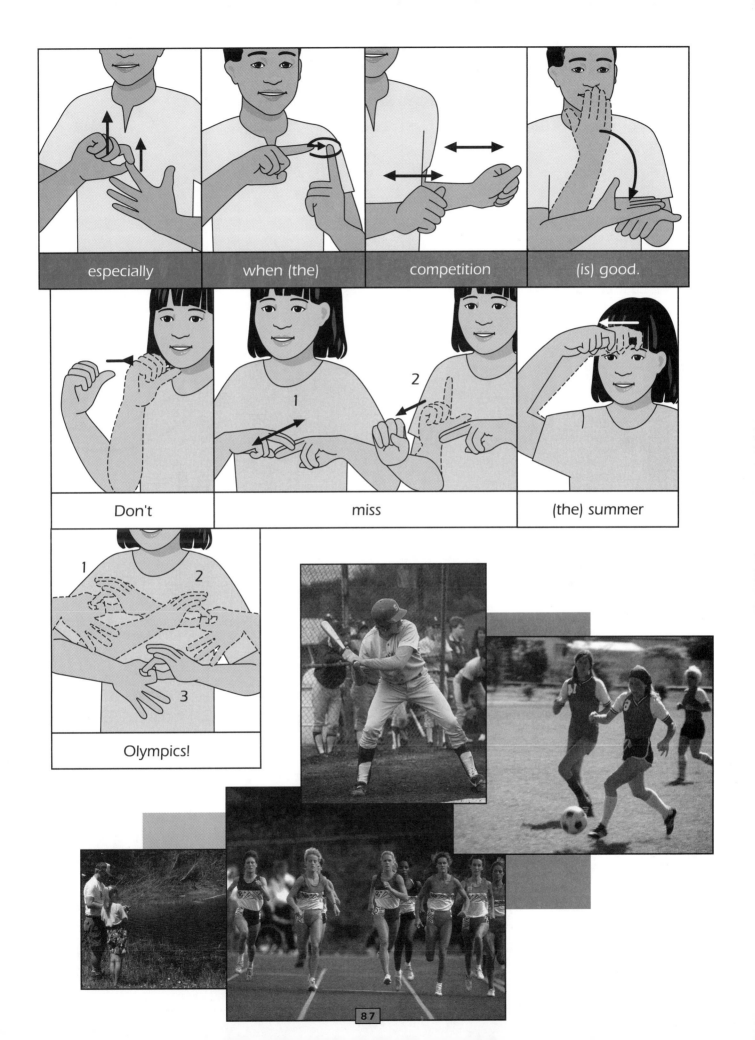

especially	when (the)	competition	(is) good.

Don't	miss	(the) summer

Olympics!

Sports:

The following sport signs closely mimic the actual sports. Match each sport with its sign.

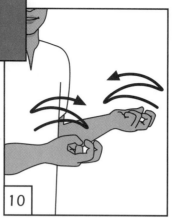

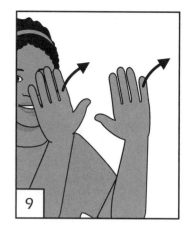

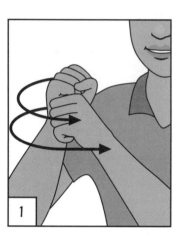

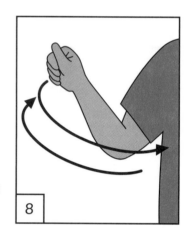

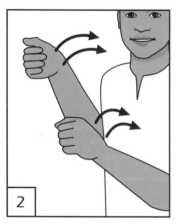

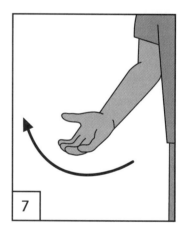

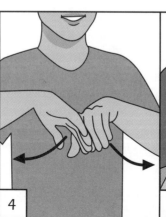

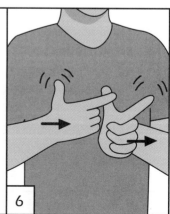

Months:

Match the months with the signs. Months of the year follow a pattern. You were introduced to September and October in this lesson. How are March–May and June–July, months beginning with the same letters, handled?

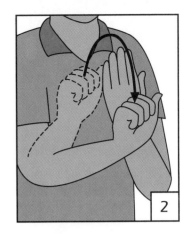

May

February

December

January

July

April

March

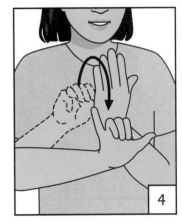

August

June

NOVEMBER

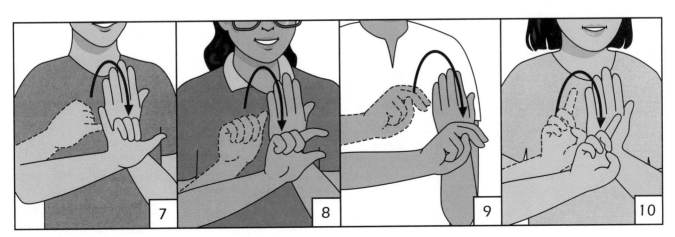

Chapter 11

Special Occasions

My	family	celebrate(s)
special	occasion(s).	Many
(of) our		
celebration(s)	(are the) Jewish	tradition(s),	Hanukkah

and	Passover.	We	celebrate

(the) Christian	tradition(s),	Christmas

and	Easter.	Everyone (every person)

enjoy(s)	(a) birthday	party!

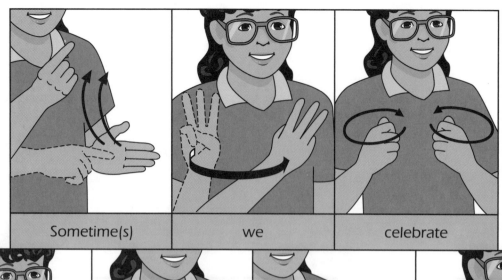

Sometime(s)	we	celebrate

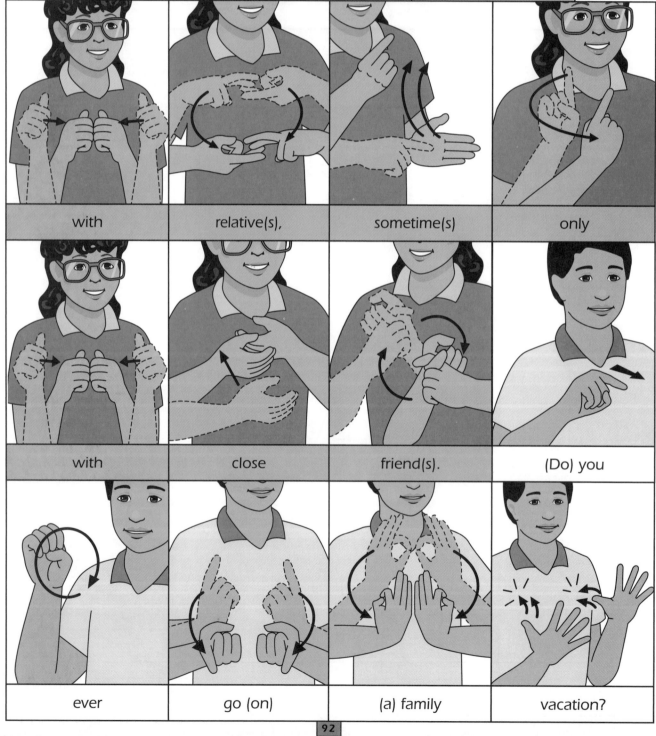

with	relative(s),	sometime(s)	only

with	close	friend(s).	(Do) you

ever	go (on)	(a) family	vacation?

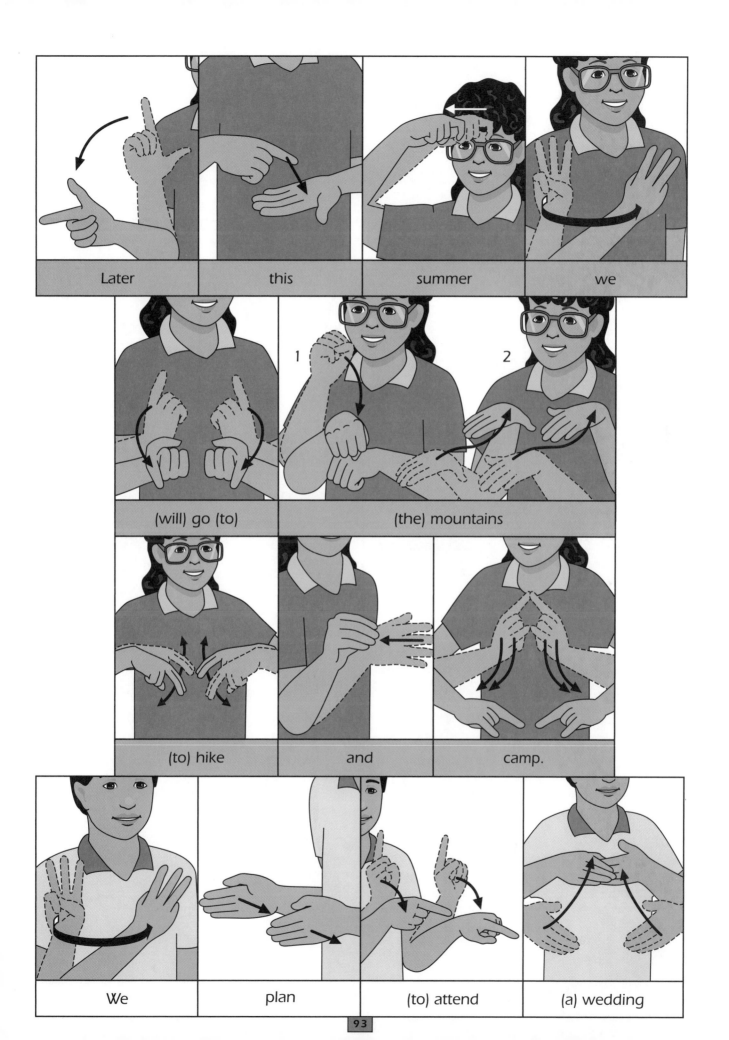

Later	this	summer	we

(will) go (to)	(the) mountains	

(to) hike	and	camp.

We	plan	(to) attend	(a) wedding

just	before	Valentine's	Day.
I	hope	(the) celebration	has
(an) interpreter!	(Do) you	have	(any) favorite
holiday(s)?	I	always	like

October	and	November	because (of)
Halloween	and	Thanksgiving.	I
like	any	holiday	when
I	don't	have	school!

95

Related Signs:

Letters of two related words are combined. Unscramble the letters to make words and then match the unscrambled pairs with their signs. Several signs should be familiar to you. Other signs show enough visual clues for you to identify them.

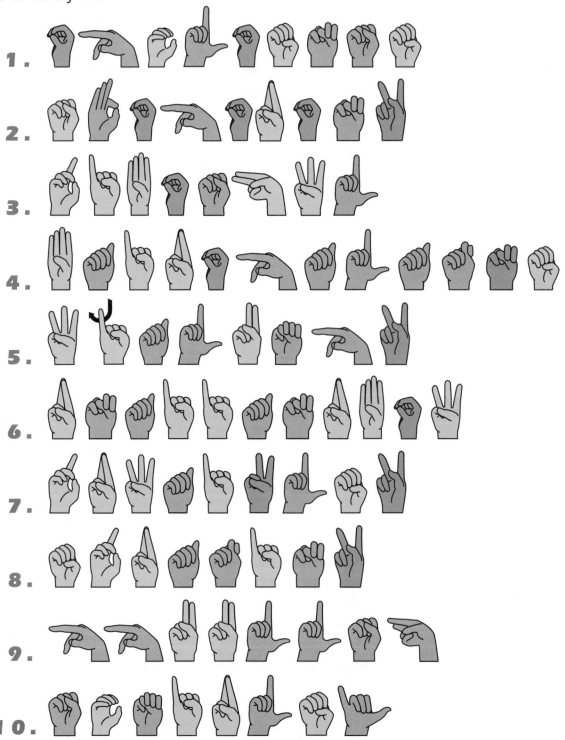

1.

2.

3.

4.

5.

6.

7.

8.

9.

10.

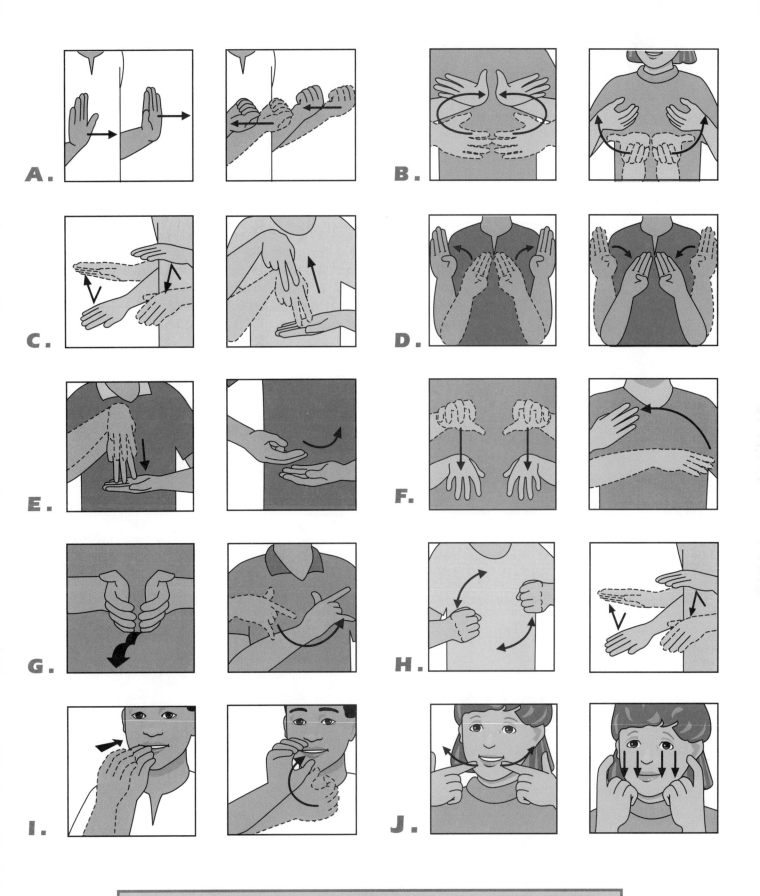

A.

B.

C.

D.

E.

F.

G.

H.

I.

J.

Some signs are very graphic. These pairs of signs have been chosen because they clearly demonstrate their meaning.

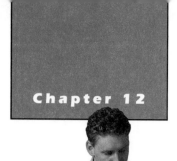

Chapter 12

In an Emergency Situation

Emergency situations require important decisions. An emergency situation might involve an injury, an illness, a fire, or an accident. What should you do in an emergency situation? Here are some suggestions:

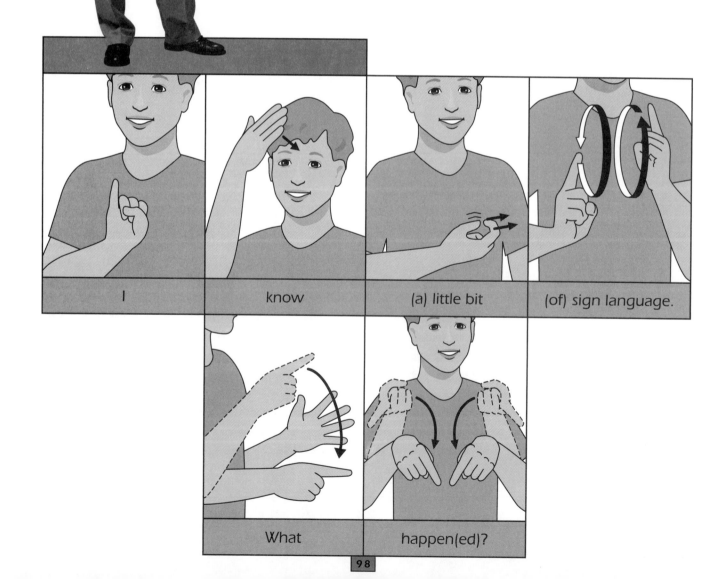

I	know	(a) little bit	(of) sign language.

What	happen(ed)?

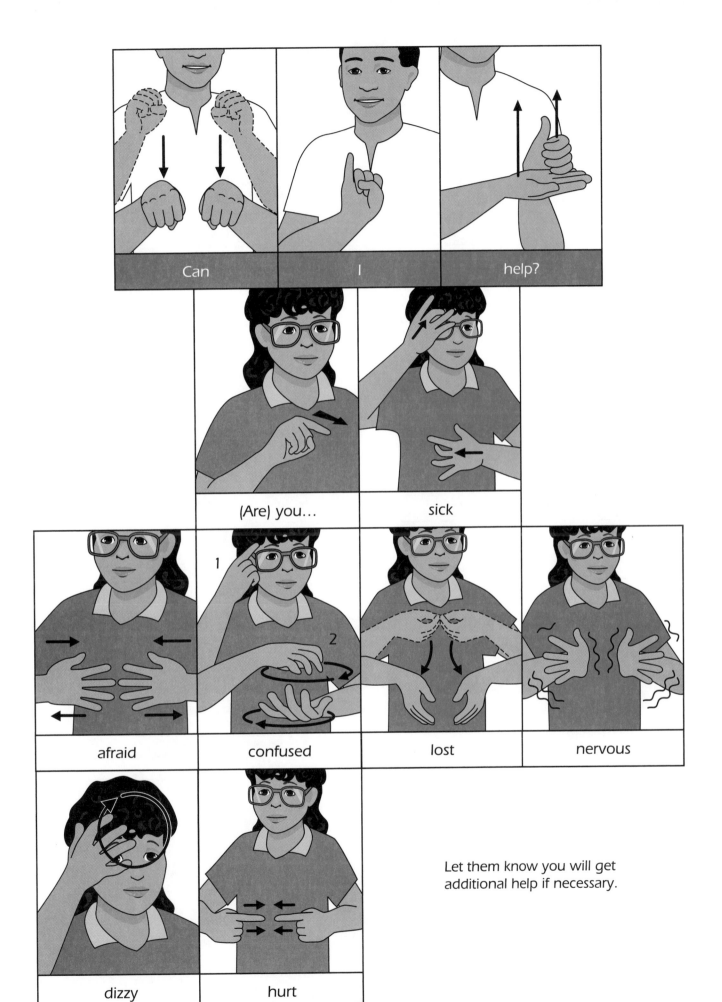

Can

I

help?

(Are) you...

sick

afraid

confused

lost

nervous

dizzy

hurt

Let them know you will get additional help if necessary.

| I | (will) telephone: |

| 9 | 1 | 1 |

firefighter (fire + person)

minister (preach + person)

police officer (police + person)

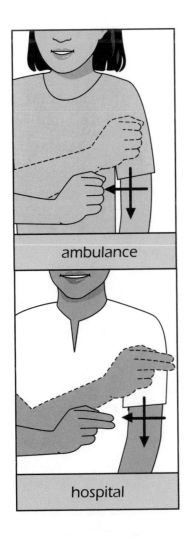

ambulance

hospital

Call 911 or dial Operator to ask for help. State that a person is hearing impaired and they will need an interpreter.

Giving directions is often necessary to help someone.

Directions should be short and to the point. This is very important in an emergency situation when someone is hurt or sick. Here are helpful phrases and directions.

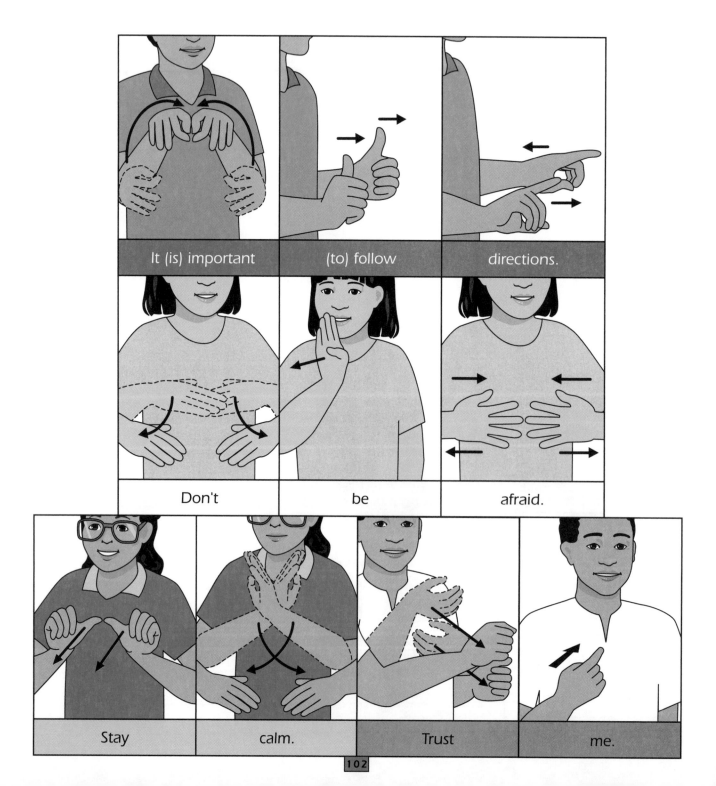

It (is) important	(to) follow	directions.
Don't	be	afraid.
Stay	calm.	Trust	me.

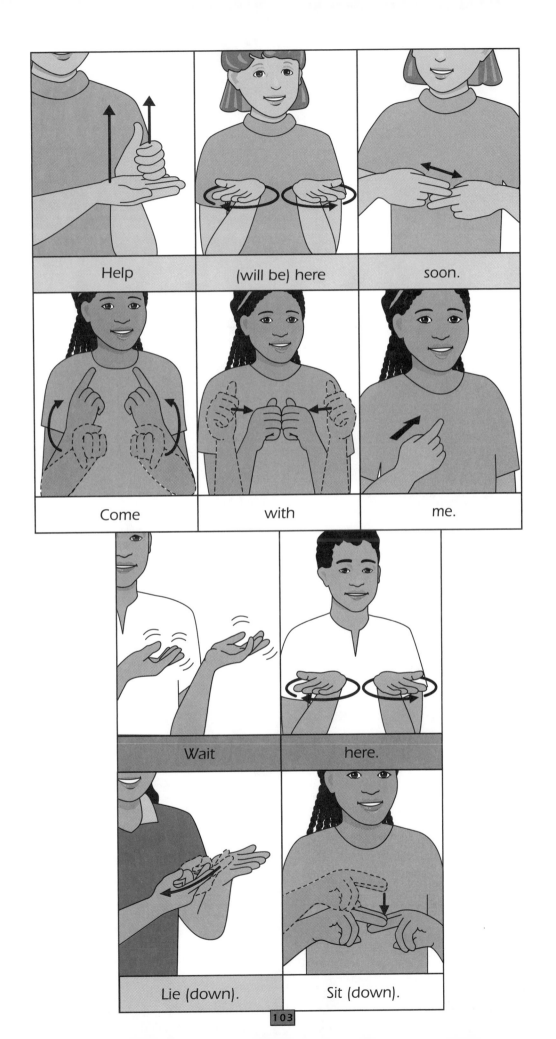

Help (will be) here soon.

Come with me.

Wait here.

Lie (down). Sit (down).

People:

You may have noticed how sign language often treats a job or a person's identity. A firefighter is signed as "fire person," a sign made from "fire" and "person." Minister is similar, made from "preach" and "person." Knowing this, can you identify these occupations?

A. musician

B. architect

C. student

D. chef

E. pilot

F. postal worker

G. police officer

H. librarian

a. police person

b. fly person

c. library person

d. house person

e. stamp person

f. cook person

g. music person

h. study person

1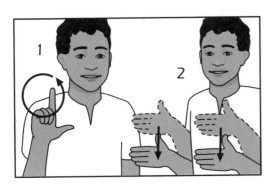

2

3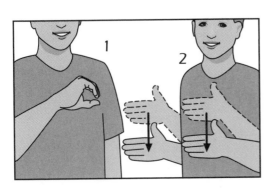

4

5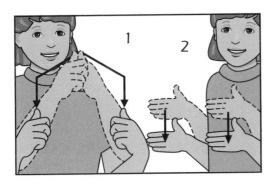

6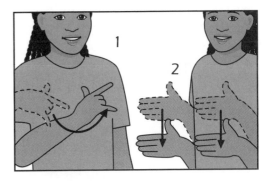

7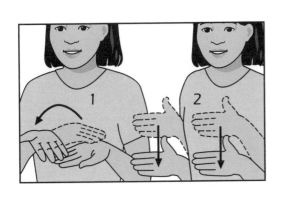

8

Index

little bit 98
live 20
look 49
lost 99
lunch 32
M 12
make 35
mall 53
many 27
March 89
match 55
math 72
May 89
maybe 29
me 22
meal 38
mean 72
meat 42
medicine 47
meet 6
might 37
milk 36
million 34
minister 101
minute 33
miss 87
Monday 34
money 54
more 23
morning 32
mother 27
mountains 93
mouse 67
movie 30
much 77
music 73
musician 105
my 16
mystery 60
N 13
name 16
nauseous 49
near 20
neck 50
necklace 57
need 47
neighbor 29
nervous 99
new 52
newspaper 54
nice 24
night 37
no 22
north 21
nose 44
not 43
November 89

number 32
nurse 43
O 13
occasion 90
October 89
OK 48
old 22
Olympics 87
one 34
only 92
open 97
or 30
orange 42
our 29
owl 69
P 13
pair 56
pants 54
paper 74
parent 71
party 55
Passover 91
peach 42
pear 42
penguin 69
people 28
person 78
pet 63
phone 32
pig 67
piglet 70
pill 47
pilot 104
pink 64
plan 93
plate 36
play 41
please 23
police officer 101
pony 70
postal worker 105
potato 37
practice 23
pull 97
puppy 70
purple 65
purse 62
push 97
Q 13
R 14
rabbit 68
rain 97
rainbow 97
raincoat 62
reading 75
ready 60
red 64

relative 92
report 75
research 74
restaurant 39
return 48
ride 30
rollerskating 88
run 41
running 88
S 14
salad 41
sale 54
same 73
sandwich 36
Saturday 31
save 54
school 71
science 73
search (look for) 56
season 85
second 33
see 24
September 89
she 29
sheep 66
shirt 54
shoe 55
shop 52
shopping 52
shot 47
should 39
sick 43
sign 23
sign language 73
silver 56
similar (same) 74
sister 22
sit 35
skirt 55
sky 78
sleep 49
slow 23
slowly 23
small 33
smell 78
smile 97
snack 42
snake 68
snow 80
soccer 84
socks 55
soda 36
sometimes 92
soon 103
soup 41
special 56
spend 61

spider 69
spoon 40
sport 82
spring 33
start 39
stay 102
stomach 44
stomachache 44
stop 25
street 20
student 74
study 73
subject 73
suit 62
summer 40
sun 81
Sunday 34
sweater 62
swim 78
T 14
talk 32
tan 65
teach 72
teacher 73
team 83
telephone (to call) 100
telephone 30
ten 34
tennis 88
thank 23
Thanksgiving 95
that 55
think 21
thirsty 35
this 57
thousand 34
throat 44
throw 78
throw up 49
Thursday 34
tiger 68
time 24
tiny 33
tired 41
to 6
toast 42
tomorrow 32
tonight 30
too 22
touch 79
town 21
tradition 90
travel 60
tree 79
trip 59
trust 102
Tuesday 34

turtle 63
twelve 22
two 80
U 14
umbrella 62
uncle 59
use 76
V 14
vacation 92
Valentine 94
vegetable 37
very 46
vest 62
volleyball 88
vomit 49
W 15
wait 103
walk 30
wallet 62
want 45
warm 81
wash 49
watch (look) 49
watch 49
water 40
we 29
wedding 93
Wednesday 34
week 48
well 23
were 6
what 19
when 75
where 6
which 71
white 64
will 54
winter 33
with 38
wonder 38
wonderful 59
work 77
world 39
worry 45
wrist watch 57
write 75
writing 74
X 15
Y 15
year 85
yellow
yes 20
you 6
your 19
Z 15
zebra 67

Chapter 3

Page 10

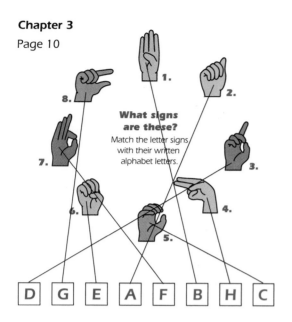

What signs are these?

Match the letter signs with their written alphabet letters.

D G E A F B H C

Page 11

1. <u>F</u> <u>E</u> <u>D</u>   2. <u>F</u> <u>A</u> <u>C</u> <u>E</u>

3. <u>H</u> <u>E</u> <u>A</u> <u>D</u>   4. <u>B</u> <u>A</u> <u>G</u>

5. <u>H</u> <u>A</u> <u>D</u>   6. <u>A</u> <u>C</u> <u>E</u> <u>D</u>

7. <u>D</u> <u>E</u> <u>A</u> <u>F</u>   8. <u>C</u> <u>A</u> <u>B</u>

Page 12

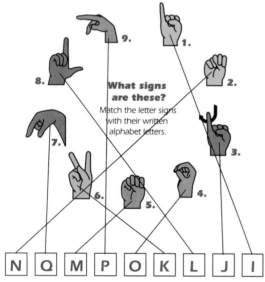

What signs are these?

Match the letter signs with their written alphabet letters.

N Q M P O K L J I

Page 13

1. <u>M</u> <u>I</u> <u>L</u> <u>K</u>   2. <u>M</u> <u>O</u> <u>P</u>

3. <u>P</u> <u>I</u> <u>N</u>   4. <u>J</u> <u>O</u> <u>I</u> <u>N</u>

5. <u>P</u> <u>I</u> <u>L</u> <u>L</u>   6. <u>J</u> <u>I</u> <u>M</u>

7. <u>I</u> <u>N</u> <u>K</u>   8. <u>M</u> <u>O</u> <u>O</u> <u>N</u>

Page 14

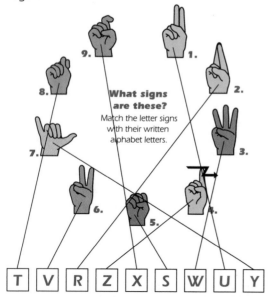

What signs are these?

Match the letter signs with their written alphabet letters.

T V R Z X S W U Y

Page 15

1. <u>T</u> <u>U</u> <u>X</u>   2. <u>R</u> <u>U</u> <u>S</u> <u>T</u>

3. <u>S</u> <u>U</u> <u>Z</u> <u>Y</u>   4. <u>S</u> <u>T</u> <u>Y</u>

5. <u>T</u> <u>R</u> <u>Y</u>   6. <u>Y</u> <u>U</u> <u>R</u> <u>T</u>

Chapter 3
Pages 25-26
1. Stepbrothers
2. Just between you and me
3. Reading between the lines
4. Stop in the Name of Love
5. Scrambled eggs
6. Ants in his pants
7. Spiral notebook
8. Square dance
9. Mixed up kid
10. Eggs over easy

Chapter 4
Pages 33-34
Themes and sequential order may vary slightly.
1. Theme: seasons
   fall (autumn)
   winter
   spring
   summer
2. Theme: size
   elephant
   cow
   chicken
   bee
3. Theme: time
   second
   minute
   hour
   day
4. Theme: size
   tiny
   small
   large
   huge
5. Theme: Family Order
   mother
   father
   grandfather
   great grandmother
6. Theme: Numbers
   one
   ten
   hundred
   thousand
   million
7. Theme: Days of the Week
   Sunday
   Monday
   Tuesday
   Wednesday
   Thursday
   Friday
   Saturday

Chapter 5
Pages 40-42
Common features may vary.
1. Common: milk, juice, water. (Liquids). Food.
2. Common: morning, afternoon, night. (Periods of the Day). Tomorrow.
3. Common: fall, summer, winter (Periods of the Year). Sunday.
4. Common: fork, spoon, knife (Eating Utensils). Glass.
5. Common: hungry, thirsty, tired (Physical Well Being). Family.
6. Common: sister, mother, brother (Family Members). Friend.
7. Common: ice cream, cake, cookie (Desserts). Salad.
8. Common: sandwich, hot dogs, hamburgers (Solid Foods). Soup.
9. Common: walk, play, run (Exercise). Sit.
10. Common: meat, fruit, vegetables (Food Categories). Snack.
11. Common: egg, toast, bacon (Breakfast Foods). Candy.
12. Common: orange, grapefruit, lemon (Citrus Fruits). Peach.
13. Common: car, airplane, boat (Transportation). Bird.
14. Common: apple, grape, pear (Fruits). Carrot.

Chapter 6
Pages 49-51
Part 1
1. G
2. C
3. J
4. A
5. F
6. E
7. B
8. H
9. I
10. D
Part 2
Answers may vary.
1. g or d, eye
2. e, body
3. f, head
4. a or c, neck
5. i, face
6. i, hand
7. j, leg
8. b or k, teeth
9. h, heart
10. f or j, foot

Chapter 7
Pages 61-62
Part 1: Goes together
1 socks — 10 shoes
2 pants — 7 belt
3 sell — 5 buy
4 save — 9 spend
6 skirt — 8 shirt
9 gold — 11 silver
Part 2: More go together
1 necktie — 8 suit
2 necklace — 9 bracelet
3 coat — 11 hat
4 vest — 10 sweater
5 umbrella — 12 raincoat
6 wallet — 7 purse

Chapter 8
Pages 69-70
Part 1:
Animal Signs You can Guess
1. f
2. c
3. h
4. e
5. b
6. g
7. a
8. d

Part 2: Animal Babies
1. d
2. g
3. f
4. c
5. a
5. e
7. b

Chapter 9
Pages 78-81
1. baseball : throw as football : G (kick)
2. nose : smell as finger : A (touch)
3. grass : green as sky : E (blue)
4. fish : swim as person : D (walk)
5. hotdog : eat as milk : B (drink)
6. monkey : tree as hippo : C (water)
7. shoe : sock as hand : F (glove)
8. tree : forest as water : D (lake)
9. one : two as A : B (the letter B)
10. cat : kitten as dog : G (puppy)
11. winter : snow as summer : E (sun)
12. potato : vegetable as apple : A (fruit)
13. cool : cold as warm : C (hot)

Chapter 10
Pages 88-89
Part 1: Sports
1. J
2. F
3. A
4. B
5. I
6. H
7. E
8. D
9. C
10. G
Part 2: Months
1. January
2. April
3. February
4. May
5. March
6. June
7. July
8. August
9. November
10. December

Chapter 11
Pages 96-97
1. open — close, D
2. fork — spoon, E
3. dish — bowl, B
4. boat — airplane, G
5. walk — jump, C
6. rain — rainbow, F
7. drive — walk, H
8. eat — drink, I
9. push — pull, A
10. smile — cry, J

Chapter 12
Pages 104-105
A. g, 2
B. d, 5
C. h, 4
D. f, 7
E. b, 6
F. e, 8
G. a, 3
H. c, 1

Beginning Sign Language

An Alphabet of Animal Signs
ISBN 0-931993-65-2
GP-065 • 16 pages
Animal illustrations and associated signs for each letter of the alphabet.

Can I Help? Helping the Hearing Impaired in Emergency Situations
ISBN 0-931993-57-1
GP-057 • 32 pages
Signs, sentences, and information to help communicate with the hearing impaired.

Caring for Young Children: Signing for Day Care Providers and Sitters
ISBN 0-931993-58-X
GP-058 • 32 pages
Signs for feelings, directions, activities, foods, bedtime, discipline, comfort-giving.

Finger Alphabet
ISBN 0-931993-46-6
GP-046 • 32 pages
Uses word games and activities to teach the finger alphabet.

Mother Goose in Sign
ISBN 0-931993-66-0
GP-066 • 16 pages
Illustrated Mother Goose nursery rhymes.

Number and Letter Games
ISBN 0-931993-72-5
GP-072 • 32 pages
Presents a variety of games involving the finger alphabet, sign numbers, and recognizable, graphic signs.

Signing at School
ISBN 0-931993-47-4
GP-047 • 32 pages
Presents signs needed in a school setting.

Songs in Sign
ISBN 0-931993-71-7
GP-071 • 16 pages
Presents six songs in Signed English. The easy-to-follow illustrations enable you to sign along.

Expanded Songs In Sign
ISBN 0-931993-05-9
GP-005 • 32 pages
An expansion of *Songs in Sign* to eleven songs in signed English. The easy-to-follow illustrations enable you to sign along.

Family and Community
ISBN 0-931993-73-3
GP-073 • 32 pages
View a family album and meet community workers through signs and photos.

Foods
ISBN 0-931993-87-3
GP-087 • 16 pages
A colorful collection of photos with signs for 43 common foods.

Fruits & Vegetables
ISBN 0-931993-88-1
GP-088 • 16 pages
Thirty-nine beautiful photos with signs.

Holidays & Celebrations
ISBN 0-931993-10-5
GP-010 • 32 pages
A collection of pictures and signs capturing the moments of holidays and special occasions in and about daily life.

Pets, Animals & Creatures
ISBN 0-931993-89-X
GP-089 • 32 pages
Photos and signs for 77 pets, animals, and creatures found at home, on the farm, in the forest, in the desert, in grassland, in the Arctic, and in the water.

Signing at Church
ISBN 0-931993-98-9
GP-098 • 32 pages
A collection of greetings, questions, The Lord's Prayer, a passage from John, and other illustrated signing vocabulary.

Signing at Sunday School
ISBN 0-931993-99-7
GP-099 • 32 pages
Songs, The Story of Jesus, and Bible verses all in a simple illustrated vocabulary.

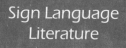

Sign Language Literature

The **Sign Language Literature Series** presents stories from different cultures. Each story uses simple language, full color art, and is complemented with illustrated signs.

Ananse the Spider: Why Spiders Stay on the Ceiling
ISBN 0-931993-85-7
GP-085 • 32 pages
A West African folk tale about the boastful spider Ananse and why spiders now hide in dark corners.

Coyote and Bobcat
ISBN 0-931993-81-4
GP-081 • 32 pages
Adapted from a Navajo story that explains how the coyote and the bobcat got their shapes.

Fountain of Youth
ISBN 0-931993-86-5
GP-086 • 32 pages
This Korean folk tale about neighbors shows the rewards of kindness and the folly of greed.

Raven and Water Monster
ISBN 0-931993-82-2
GP-082 • 32 pages
Adapted from a Haida story, it tells how raven gained his beautiful black color and how he brought water to the earth.

A Word in the Hand: Book One
ISBN 0-931993-08-3 (hardcover: ISBN 0-931993-68-7)
GP-008 • 116 pages
(hardcover: 068 • 116 pages)

A Word in the Hand: Book Two
ISBN 0-931993-40-7 (hardcover: ISBN 0-931993-69-5)
GP-040 • 92 pages
(hardcover: GP069 • 92 pages)

Basic primers to Signed English. Book One contains 15 lessons and nearly 500 illustrations. Book Two contains 10 lessons with over 300 illustrations. All lessons provide vocabulary, illustrations, review, exercises, and assignments that students and adults will find exciting.

Sound Hearing • ISBN 0-931993-26-1
GP-026 • booklet/tape

Provides listening samples to illustrate sound, hearing, and hearing loss. Listeners will hear as impaired people might, listening to music, a story, and taking a simple spelling test.

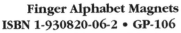

Finger Alphabet Magnets
ISBN 1-930820-06-2 • GP-106

High quality vinyl magnets, the 26 letters of the Sign Language manual alphabet, plus a bonus two extra tiles.

Finger Alphabet Cards   **Sign Number Cards**
ISBN 0-931993-09-1   **ISBN 0-931993-22-9**
GP-009 • 26 cards   **GP-022 • 20 cards**

These sturdy 8 1/2" x 11" cards provide the basics for all signing. They provide the beginner with the immediate reinforcement that spurs facility in signing.

Flash Cards

Beginning Signing Primer Cards
ISBN 0-931993-36-9
GP 036 • 100 cards (4"x6")

Perfect for young and beginning signers. Signs and vocabulary for colors, creatures, days, months, time, weather, and family members.

Basic Signing Vocabulary Cards, Set A
ISBN 0-931993-23-7
GP-023 • 100 cards (4"x6")

Basic Signing Vocabulary Cards, Set B
ISBN 0-931993-24-5
GP-024 • 100 cards (4"x6")

Each set teaches simple vocabulary and associated signs. Words are chosen from basic sight and beginning vocabulary lists and are combined with a beginning sign vocabulary.

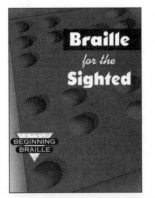

Finger Alphabet Lotto (game)
GP-048 • ISBN 0-931993-48-2
This card matching game teaches the Sign Language finger alphabet.

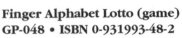

Game

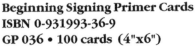

Braille

Braille for the Sighted
ISBN 0-931993-95-4
GP-095 • 32 pages
An introduction to braille for those who are sighted. Learn the alphabet and numbers to complete a variety of games and activities.